14 Days

# AFRICAN CREEKS
# I HAVE BEEN UP

## By SUE SPENCER

AFRICAN

In a letter to her college-age daughters in the United States, Sue Spencer, en route to join her engineer-husband in West Africa, wrote: "Mining engineers have always had to live in Siberias of one kind or another, and I daresay we will triumph over the vicissitudes of West Africa, even as we have over others." Thus, at the outset of years of tours of duty in Africa, interspersed with periodic terms of leave, Mrs. Spencer has stated her premise. And this is the story of how this spirited woman and her family triumphed over difficult living conditions, a wearing climate, a primitive native society, and mishaps too numerous to mention, all of which she bore with unfailing good humor.

*African Creeks I Have Been Up* has quality and style. The author's point of view is temperate and re-

*(Continued on back flap)*

# African Creeks I Have Been Up

BY SUE SPENCER

DAVID McKAY COMPANY, INC.

New York

*For Miss Ruth with love*

# Contents

# Tour I: 1956-1957

Dear Lolly and Suzy,

In spite of my new hat and first-class ticket across the Atlantic, I cried all the way to New York. It broke my heart to leave you weeping on the tarmac. I wasn't sure you were weeping for me or because I ripped that poor man's bumper off on the way to the airport. I hope he wasn't too fractious. He still seemed irate, even when I produced the Al-Gold Seal insurance policy.

Our separation is unavoidable because you must finish your education and your father must make money to pay for our necessities: a split-level in Florida, a butter warmer in the refrigerator and a boat for water-skiing. Mining engineers always have to live in Siberias of one kind or another, and I daresay we will triumph over the vicissitudes of West Africa, even as we have over Arkansas, Australia, and Alabama.

John, Tom and Rob are busy looking over the plane, turning knobs, zipping zippers, lowering seats and examining the emergency exit with a speculative eye. It was a mistake to put them near the place where a hole can be made in the aircraft. At Idlewild Airport Tom slammed the car door on his thumb and broke it. It has begun to ache now, and we have lost the pain pills. I had only half an hour in New York to change planes, weigh in our mountain of luggage, see that our passports were in order and wash a candy bar off Rob's face—then

Tom had to break his thumb. He was rushed off to a doctor who x-rayed, splinted and bandaged it in a few minutes. When we dashed through the gate, all the other passengers were aboard and the plane was roaring impatiently on the runway. Then we taxied over to a corner of the airfield and sat for an hour and a half.

There is a distinguished, ambassadorial-looking French steward on board who apparently doesn't like nine-, seven- and four-year-olds. I will reduce him to a quivering pulp by threatening to bring all my children next time.

We have just had our dinner with cuisine by Maxim. The boys take everything offered to them—cigarettes, champagne, Cointreau. I just reached across the aisle and quietly twisted John's arm to get him to abstain from some of the fleshpots.

I managed to take Tom's cigarettes away a split second before he lit up. Later, when we landed in the Azores and he saw small Spanish boys puffing away on the weed, it only confirmed his suspicion that his mother was a miserable killjoy.

You sophisticated college girls would be so much easier to travel with than your little brothers. Take care of each other. I miss you so.

Love, Mama

IN THE AIR<br>LISBON TO DAKAR

Dear Lolly and Suzy,

Early this morning we flew into Lisbon, green and beautiful with real castles on the hills. Portugal is your father's favorite country and, respecting his worldwide travel experience, we love it, though I can see that less cosmopolitan people might consider it cold, gloomy and damp. We had thick black coffee that tasted like stump water but we drank it as if it was the

4

best in the world. We stayed only long enough for the plane to change crews. Whether they changed because of us I don't know. We have had all kinds of trouble with our non-collapsible fishing poles and our eleven bags. Bob knew when he asked me to bring these poles that it was an impossible task. Every airline in the world has refused these poles and yet he is confident that I can get them through. Well, I have. The only place they fit is standing up in the ladies' room.

We are now flying toward Dakar over the edge of the Sahara Desert, but it is too dark to see a single Bedouin, mirage or oasis. I am turning these exotic words over in my mind to help pass the time while the children clamber over me for endless drinks of water and trips to the toilet. The coloring books, crayons and picture books provided by the management are a dead loss. Tom is even bored with his new broken thumb. The only things the boys enjoy while airborne are their usual fights and the constant stream of food and drink. Long before a flight is over I am satiated with food and drink, but they hold out to the end. Now they are stuffing their pockets with gifts from the less acquisitive passengers and will get off the plane bulging with mints, crackers, cheese, toothpicks, sugar and little boxes of Morton's salt.

Love, Mama

DAKAR
FRENCH WEST AFRICA

Dear Lolly and Suzy,

Bob met us here. We were so happy to see him and he, us. Why he was happy to see us takes some thought, but for me, the prospect of having another parent around made me positively ecstatic. Two parents is one of the cleverest ideas Mother Nature ever had.

5

We are staying at a beautiful, modern hotel overlooking a primitive village. Bob says this is the only way to appreciate a primitive village. Everyone speaks only French, including the waiters, who are handsome Africans in fezzes, red jackets and full, black trousers. The food is delicious and so French that the sauces have sauces. The rolls are so hard that it takes two of us to crack them. I ate snails for the first time and they are like the small coon oysters we get in the creek at Bugtussle in Florida. The chef must be rushed this week because all the food is rare—steak, chicken, pork and duck. Coffee and tea are easy to come by, but it has taken me two days to find a source of water, a large bottle called Vitelle. They will give you other things that look like water, but this is the only one that tastes right. Bob says that from now on, no water is safe unless it is boiled and filtered.

This hotel has do-it-yourself elevators which the children are frenziedly operating, trying to make as many trips as possible in the few days we are here. There are no guard doors on the cage, so each clang of the door conjures up a vision of mangled little legs. Our suite also has a lovely balcony nine stories high. Tom hangs over this railing to sail planes to John below. I hope their guardian angel knows we have moved to Africa.

Love, Mama


BATHURST, GAMBIA
BRITISH WEST AFRICA

Dear Lolly and Suzy,

Yesterday we drove to Gambia from Dakar by Land Rover. This vehicle is the English version of a jeep and is the most popular mode of transport in Africa.

Gambia is England's oldest, smallest and poorest colony.

When Elizabeth I sent a trading company there in 1588 she thought the Gambia River would be the key to open up the whole interior of Africa with its gold and ivory. Unfortunately the river led nowhere and its chief wealth lay in mosquitoes.

On coming into British territory we had our first experience with African curiosity. We had to wait all afternoon for a boat to cross the river to Bathurst and, since there was no hurry, the customs officials, all Africans, went through our luggage item by item. All the villagers crowded up for a look when something interesting was unearthed. My voluminous crinoline which I had laboriously sheathed in an old stocking caused great consternation when they pulled it out. When the people finished looking through our things, they looked at us the rest of the afternoon. Africans can look down your throat, in your pocketbook or into your bathroom window with such sang-froid that you feel like a crotchety prude if you resent such kindly interest in your affairs.

We waited all afternoon in a cold rain as the river was too rough to launch a boat until after dark. The boat finally arrived, looking like a bedraggled *African Queen*. About thirty passengers appeared from out of the dark, blending their French, Syrian, English and African accents into a terrible din as we leaped aboard the open launch. One had to leap at the moment the boat crashed into the rickety dock between waves. A huge, grinning Sudanese threw the children into the boat where they were caught by a brawny crewman in a loincloth. I was numb with cold and fright, and kept trying to remember how I got there. John, Tom, Rob and the other primitives chattered and laughed and seemed to enjoy the harrowing twenty-mile crossing.

Normally there is a ferry that makes this crossing, but it had capsized a few weeks before, drowning ninety people.

I was so glad to be ashore I will always remember Bathurst with affection. We stayed in a small modern hotel with excellent service. The town itself reminded me of St. Augustine, Florida without all the terrible neon tourist signs. After a delicious dinner we fell exhausted into bed, under mosquito nets for the first time. I like nets. I don't know about their keeping mosquitoes out but they do help to keep small boys in.

Love, Mama

Dear Lolly and Suzy,

None of the Europeans I have met considers himself a resident of West Africa. He is always on a tour of duty. You are asked how many tours you have done or what is the length of your tour. Most of the English civil servants stay in Africa eighteen months and then have three months leave in England. The American missionaries do a three-year tour and the Catholic nuns and fathers stay for five years without going home. The tendency nowadays is for shorter leaves and shorter tours. Our company has a policy of unheard-of leniency—ten-month tours with two months leave.

Your father is doing some consulting work here for an English company that is mining rutile. This is the same mineral that he was mining in Australia. It is heavy black sand that is used for making paint pigment and titanium metal. We will be in Gambia for several months before we go to Sierra Leone, our ultimate destination, where we will do further prospecting for rutile. Americans pronounce rutile to rhyme with heel but the British use a long *i* and it rhymes with tile. Diamond-mining is the big business in Sierra Leone, and I wish we were looking for gems instead of black sand.

Our house is comfortable, with electricity, plumbing and

four servants. Your father says I am getting a distorted view of the real West Africa by such posh living but this will be corrected when I get to the bush of Sierra Leone. One does hear such horrible tales of deadly snakes that hang from trees, of incurable diseases and of tribes that practice human sacrifice. During the day I have no qualms but at night if I happen to awaken, I toss and think of my usual worries—bills to be paid, the atom bomb, unkind words I have said—and now of the hazards of Africa as well.

I am awakened each morning by a fierce-looking African lifting up the mosquito net saying, "Tea, Madam." The first few times I nearly jumped out of my skin but now I am a devotee of the custom. The servants, all men, still serve in the same way they were taught by the Victorians, using every dish and piece of silver that it is possible to get on the table. Even at breakfast there is an array of several knives, forks and spoons, all slightly greasy. There are no paper napkins, so for even the smallest snack, we use heavy linen damask ones, usually spotted from yesterday's food. No one minds a little dirt; the style is the thing. At dinner we are served soup, fish, meat, vegetables, a sweet (desserts are called sweets), a savory or cheese and crackers. I mean cheese and biscuits. Crackers are firecrackers to English people.

An Englishman's eating ritual is sacred and he is appalled at the casual way Americans treat food. We went on a picnic with a couple who took dinner knives and forks, dessert knives and forks and fish knives and forks. Bob and I felt very gauche with only one knife and fork each. I think they eat with ceremony so they won't notice the taste of the food. The kindest thing that can be said for English food is that it is harmless to children.

Bob has been among foreigners so long that he has been brain-washed and likes to have a five-course dinner each evening at eight thirty. How will I ever get to PTA meetings on time when we come home?

Each morning I put the day's food out for the cook, saying, "This is meat, this is vegetable, etc." Most of the food comes in cans and the cook cannot read the labels. If the cans get mixed we are liable to have plums for a vegetable and ripe olives for dessert. Africans don't eat our food so they don't know how things should taste. That is why I maintain that it is impossible to get a good African cook. Often things look right but they never taste right. My neighbor's cook made a delicious banana pudding for her, but through a slight misunderstanding, he put a layer of Brussels sprouts on the top.

The servants speak a little English but no American. My Alabama accent is incomprehensible to them. The children have quickly adopted a pseudo-British accent and are communicating very well. It is too late by several decades to do anything about my accent but I have learned a few words to use with my English friends—lorry, fridge, petrol, wireless and joint (roast). One kind neighbor advised me to "keep my pecker up no matter how frustrating things become." She meant for me to be of good cheer. I have so much to learn.

Love, Mama

DAY AFTER CHRISTMAS
GAMBIA

Dear Lolly and Suzy,

Today is Boxing Day, the traditional English holiday when one is supposed to take boxes to the poor. (I always thought it had something to do with the Boxer Rebellion.) This is such a sensible holiday for soothing your conscience and clearing up the house at the same time.

We had a very sad Christmas because we were separated from you for the first time. We decorated a palm tree covered with thorns which scratched us from end to end. It is astonishing to live in this green jungle and yet be unable to find a substitute for a Christmas tree. Every tree wilts as soon as you bring it in the house. Oh, to be at Bugtussle among my cedars, pines and holly.

Our English friends want to know why ever do we call our Florida estate Bugtussle. We tell them that a half-hour visit there with the mosquitoes, ticks and cockroaches would make it abundantly clear.

The most memorable thing to write you is that we bought a turkey with the entrails frozen within. Surely it can't be good economics to ship turkey guts all the way from England. That space should have been filled with cranberries or Christmas-tree balls. The best thing about the holiday in Africa is that we spent the day on the beach in our front yard. The beach is miles long with trees growing almost to the water's edge. There are patches of boulders here and there which appeal to us Floridians who are used to only sand. We find many beautiful shells and occasionally a cowrie shell. The Africans formerly used these as currency.

Several baobab trees grow in front of the house. These are huge barrel-like trees which are often hollow and make fine houses for John, Tom and Rob. They and the monkeys also relish the fruit of the tree which is called monkey bread, a large pod filled with tart white pulp. The Africans all eat the fruit when there is a famine. The servants are afraid of baobab trees and tell Rob that a Ninky-Nanky lives in them. A Ninky-Nanky is a "plenty bad devil." We are beginning to see how every action of the African is rooted in superstition. Rob got a bag of plastic miniatures for Christmas and I have noticed the garden boy furtively toting them off. Bob says he will sell them to the medicine man who will make charms out of them. One of Bob's laborers was narrowly missed by a heavy monkey wrench which fell off a scaffold. The next day he came to work with a charm around his neck to protect him from such hazards. It was a small monkey wrench carved out of wood and blessed by the medicine man.

Rob got another present which is liable to rock the economic foundations of the country—a big bundle of Confederate play money. He left the bundle on the beach and a brisk wind scattered it for miles. Now every time I look out I see an African pouncing on a banknote and dashing off in a happy trance. The frauds that will be perpetrated are shocking to contemplate.

Love, Mama

GAMBIA<br>JANUARY

Dear Lolly and Suzy,

Happy New Year. I hope you have resolved to write me lots of letters. I wish you had some of my time. I have nothing to do but write letters and go to market.

Now that I am used to the smell, I adore the Bathurst market. Africans love to bargain and one should never pay the first price asked for things because it is at least twice what they expect to get. We are getting adept at haggling for things. There are no paper bags or wrapping paper, so I shop with a wicker basket, dripping meat on the bottom, oranges, eggs, peanuts and bananas layered on as I buy them. Cigarette tins, the size of our standard measuring cup, are the most important property of West African commerce. Everything is measured in this tin—rice, peanuts, palm oil, palm wine, salt and kola nuts.

A big, bloody carcass of beef hangs in the market surrounded by dogs, children, flies and customers. When a mangy sniffing dog gets too close, the butcher gives him a resounding thwack on the rump with the flat side of his cutlass and continues cutting meat with the sharp side. The African distaste for regularity is well illustrated by the butcher. Unlike the American butcher, he has no dull routine to follow but simply cuts chunks off the animal at random. To ease the pain of arithmetic he always has the weight come out in even pounds. I may be buying steak and he will drop in an odd piece of kidney or tongue to round off the weight. All cuts of meat cost the same, one shilling six pence (twenty-one cents). Whether one gets filet or shank bone depends on how early one gets to market. Liver, tongue and kidney are called offal, which I think is awful. I like all three of these things but I don't like them called offal.

A woman told me that this is a particularly good time of year for fruits and vegetables and that I mustn't be misled by the current opulence of the market. The only kinds of produce one can always depend on buying in West Africa are kola nuts, mangoes and foo-foo. Kola nuts are a beautiful pinkish-purple nut about the size of chestnuts, and they taste like green persimmons. They are a mild narcotic which the natives nibble all day to keep them from feeling hungry—a sort of poor man's tranquilizer. To offer kola nuts to a stranger is a sign of friendship—like our "have a Coke."

Mangoes grow everywhere on trees as big as oaks. Some are juicy and sweet and others taste like turpentine. In Florida mangoes cost a quarter each but here you get two dozen for a quarter.

Foo-foo is made of cassava, a white tuber shaped like a sweet potato which is almost pure starch. The cassava is cut up and put under water for a few days until it begins to rot, then it is dried, pounded into flour, made into small balls and sent to market. The balls look like snowballs and taste like nothing, slightly fermented. Tasteless though it is, foo-foo is as dear to the hearts of West Africans as grits are to Alabamians. (It is hard to believe, but I have heard Yankees say that they thought grits were lacking in flavor.)

Watching the people in the market is as interesting as shopping. Biblical-looking Arab traders sell native art made in Hong Kong. Handsome Mauretanian gentlemen in full beards and flowing robes walk along holding hands. Stately Jollof women float by in yards of gay material with a final covering of pastel organdy. This tribe has the most elegant ladies in all Africa. It is rumored that they keep their husbands' noses to the grindstone more than American women. A Jollof woman's dowry is her gold jewelry, which she wears as earrings or as bangles strung across her forehead. She wears intricate artificial coiffures made of buns and plaits of black wool. Her cheeks are handsomely patterned with tribal scars. These scars are made by cutting the skin and rubbing in some caustic agent to irritate the wound and cause a fine scar. One such irritant is the outer covering of the cashew nut.

This is the principal use the Africans make of this delectable nut. Cashews have a smooth, orange, pear-shaped fruit with the nut sticking out from the base. I never saw the seed of anything growing on the outside before. The fruit tastes like a muscadine, juicy and edible. The reason that the Africans don't eat the nut is that it is too much trouble. I heartily agree with them. John and I cooked and stirred a big panful over a charcoal fire all afternoon and our total profit was about six nuts. The only way to get to the delicious kernel is to burn off the sticky, poisonous outer skin in a slow fire and extract the nut the exact moment it is done. The majority of our cashews were charred beyond redemption.

I must go and help the cook because the steward boy has quit. It is rumored that he gathered up a big bundle of Rob's

Confederate money and has gone to his native village in the interior to retire.

Love, Mama

Dear Lolly and Suzy,

The most exciting event of Gambian history occurred yesterday when the Duke of Edinburgh called in on his way home from Antarctica. All of Bathurst was painted and polished beyond belief, just like the time Roosevelt visited Arkansas, and all the houses facing the road were whitewashed. People were dressed in beautiful colors, and there was much singing and dancing. A scruffy old camel and his driver had come in from the desert to greet the Duke. Maybe he came from Timbuctoo which is only a few hundred miles from Gambia.

The population of Gambia is so small that even I got an invitation to the Royal Enclosure to hear the address of welcome. With his golden beard and his sparkling white naval uniform, Philip was so breathtaking that my hands shook, spoiling the pictures I was trying to take. Everyone says his wife will make him shave his splendid beard as soon as he gets home. He walked around town, thoughtfully being available to everyone's camera, talking to the school children and being a highly successful salesman for England. If he is ever unemployed our State Department should hire him. I can't imagine anyone carrying a placard saying "Philip Go Home."

I am writing before I start my school for the day. There are no suitable schools here, so I will have to teach the boys myself. Sending small boys off for the day when they reach the age of six is one of the most succulent fruits of civilization but, alas, one I cannot now enjoy. I am struggling desperately to

15

educate them around the dining-room table, but it is discouraging. With the refrigerator in reach, the warm Atlantic lapping at the front yard and the trees full of chattering monkeys, even Socrates would have inattentive scholars.

I console myself by counting the things they learn which their contemporaries in the United States miss: how to make tribal scars, how to make rope out of palm fronds, which roots are edible during the hungry season. As the world learns better and better ways to destroy everything modern, the stone-age man will have an advantage.

Lolly, I am glad you are happy at the University of Alabama but I want to warn you that Alabama is a backward, under-developed country. As an eighth-generation Southerner, I consider myself an authority on and an example of poverty and ignorance so you must attend when I warn you of the pitfalls. Your father is a Yankee, so let that give you strength to view with a suspicious eye all the mores and folkways of Alabama—the good food, the soft talk, the balmy air. Keep a level head on your shoulders. It is too late for me: I am an Alabamian and I like it but one aspires to something better for one's children.

Love, Mama

GAMBIA<br>FEBRUARY

Dear Lolly and Suzy,

I have had no letters for a long time. There are only two planes a week scheduled to stop in Bathurst and often they don't arrive. Only two ships a month call so we are always running short of things, flour, toilet paper, sugar and potatoes. But Gambia never runs out of beer. The ships' main cargo is beer in huge green bottles. Why don't they put it in cans so they could carry twice as much in the same space? It must be as uneconomic to haul beer bottles as it is to haul turkey entrails.

In West Africa the men drink beer, the children drink squash and the ladies drink tea. Squash is a bottled syrupy fruit essence which one mixes with water. We have tea every afternoon at four o'clock, usually with some of our neighbors and sometimes served by the cook on the beach from a thermos jug. Ice is never served in anything. I have even heard conscientious English housewives apologize for things from the fridge being too cold. Iced drinks are bad for the stomach. Some day the Spencers are going to lock the door, draw the blinds and have iced tea.

No, the servants don't eat from our table. They don't care for European food except fats and sugar.

All white people in Africa are called Europeans. Rob is very upset at this foreign appellation. He keeps saying that he is an American but the cook insists that all white men are Europeans. Rob also spends hours trying to tell the cook that "to chop" means to cut. Food is called "chop" by the Africans and "to chop" means to eat. If you want the cook to serve nuts and canapés with drinks you say, "Pass small chop."

The servants cook their food in the back yard in a three-legged, black iron pot. Their favorite meal is rice served with a sauce of hot peppers, dried fish and palm oil. The men eat first, then the women and children, all without implements and from a communal pan. But it is done neatly and with decorum.

Our servants are all Moslems which are the best kind. The theory is that they abstain from palm wine and they also don't steal as much of your cooking fat, especially if you use lard. Moslems do not eat pork in any way. This is not because they consider it unclean but because a pig once saved Mohammed's life by leading him to water. The Moslems have just been celebrating the fast of Ramadan, fasting from sunrise to sunset during the holy month. Not even their spit must pass their throats so they have been spitting right and left. Our house is built up on high pillars and every time I look under the house one of the servants is praying, facing Mecca and bobbing up and down, touching his forehead to his prayer mat.

Bob and I have bought a copy of the Koran to learn something about Islam. Islam, which means submission, is a religion of a sacred book, the Koran. This book is the Moslem's law book as well as his social and military code. It is the sole textbook for most of the Moslem schools. No wonder their schools are so backward. The Koran is so repetitious I couldn't wade through it.

Islam is very attractive to the pagan Africans as it is a faith adapted to the needs of the average man. It doesn't make the excessive demand of Christianity for a complete reform or rebirth but is easygoing and somewhat akin to the tribal ways because it permits polygamy and the wearing of charms.

Gambia is more Moslem than Sierra Leone because it is on the border of North Africa which has always been hostile to Christian missionaries. Islam is a very intolerant religion and that is probably one of its chief strengths. Bob said that the Moslem countries in the United Nations refused to sign the Declaration of Human Rights because it affirmed man's right to change his religion. This was against Koranic law.

I am glad that I was not born into the Moslem religion. Camels are treated with more deference than women.

Suzy, you are a clever girl to be able to look after our accounts. Your father is so happy to have a female in the family who can make a checkbook balance.

Love, Mama

Dear Lolly and Suzy,

Your father must go to London before going to Sierra
Leone and he is going to take us with him tra-la tra-la. This
will be the first time we have ever taken a long trip together.
I have always "followed with the children."

We will go by Spain and spend a few days with your Uncle
Joe. He *has* invited us, never dreaming that we would be
passing through Madrid. His spacious apartment, his car and
his fluent Spanish make him an irresistible target. We will
send a cable announcing our arrival and he will never be able
to get one back to West Africa in time to stop us. Communications are so mercifully slow here.

We left home with a wardrobe suitable for the tropics and
I don't know how I can make it do for a European trek. I
hate to buy many warm clothes as we are coming back to
Africa soon. Perhaps you had better do up a bundle for Britain
and send it to the London office. Send a few of my warm
sweaters that you appropriated on my departure.

Nothing is too good for your father when he travels on an
expense account and, alone, he blends unobtrusively with the
international set in the best hotels. He is such a quiet, reserved
gentleman. But John, Tom and Rob don't blend—they clash—
and this trip is bound to be fraught with pain for your father.

I have noticed a paucity of small boys in the international
set. When the tray crashed in mid-aisle on the flight to
Lisbon, when the bidet flooded the bathroom in Dakar, when
the medicine man lost his ju-ju in Gambia, I always looked
hopefully for strange culprits, but I found only little Spencers.

A bidet is a fascinating piece of continental plumbing which
has followed the European to Africa. It is a low bowl, resem-
bling a toilet, which is used by ladies for their personal ablu-

tions. I have never been able to explain it successfully to the boys but the novelty of it attracts them the instant we go into a European household. They have various uses for it, as a urinal or for washing their feet or for sailing small boats. We have so much to learn.

We have shipped several boxes off to Sierra Leone—toys and treasures we have collected here—snakeskins, baskets and seashells. Have you noticed that toys never fit compactly in anything? For years I have tried without success to pack footballs, badminton rackets, roller skates, and pogo sticks into neat parcels.

Lolly, please stop falling in love so often. I realize that you are majoring in biology but I want you to get a firm foundation in theory before you start any practical application.

Love, Mama

# Three Months Later

Dear Lolly and Suzy,

Thank heavens we are back in Africa and on our way to Sierra Leone. We have been in England for three months and I froze spiritually and physically from the moment I arrived until the moment I left. No wonder Pocahontas turned up her toes and died when John Rolfe took her to London. Making friends in London is about as easy as growing watermelons in the Sahara. I will admit that I had a poorly planned wardrobe for the cold but even in a mink parka I would have shaken like a hound dog. Did you know that coal was still rationed in London? Neither did I. My neighbor used to look askance at the roaring fire in my flat. I realized something was amiss but I thought it was because I was using a broiler pan for a coal scuttle. Only when I had used up my month's ration in a week did the helpful porter give me the news about rationing. There was only one radiator in our "centrally heated" flat and it was in the hall where it maintained a steady temperature just right for a butter warmer.

There are only three warm places in London—the Savoy Hotel, the launderettes and the reptile house at the zoo. For some reason I spent very little time at the Savoy but I took the children to the zoo every time they mentioned it. While they looked at the wild animals from Africa I sat in the reptile house and basked with the kraits and cobras and one nice old rattler from Texas.

23

The coldest place in Europe was the Escorial in Spain. This is a huge, icy, stone monastery built by Philip II and where most of the Spanish kings are buried. Tom was upset when he found there were still some empty tombs and no kings left. I told him that some could be found in Portugal to fill in the blank spaces. He loves symmetry.

We left London this morning, had lunch in Bordeaux and are spending the night in Tangier.

This is the first time we have seen veiled ladies. To pass the time flying down, I told the boys tales of interest about this age-old Sodom, this haunt of murderers, smugglers and pirates. I must have overdone it because now they are cowering in the hotel, afraid to come bathing with me in the Straits of Gibraltar. We must get in our swim now because the children fall asleep immediately after dinner. I have stopped struggling with European waiters over the serving of wine to small fry. It is such a help to have drowsy, happy children when traveling.

Thanks for the Mother's Day card. I realize that time and distance have dimmed your recollection of me but I love to hear those sweet sentiments all the same.

Love, Mama

VILLA CISNEROS<br>SPANISH SAHARA

Dear Lolly and Suzy,

We have just flown over the Sahara Desert in daylight and it is a beige, wrinkled expanse of nothing with one-half an inhabitant per square mile. We also flew over the Atlas Mountains again. On the way to London the children saw snow here for the first time. Poor little Floridians having to come to Morocco to see snow.

We have stopped several times for refueling. Landing and taking off are John and Tom's favorite kind of flying. I always expect to crash each time I land. I am full of joyous disbelief when we come to a complete stop. I always keep a stiff upper lip for the children, looking calm and relaxed while we lurch through the worst air pockets. Sometime I am going to take a trip alone so I can turn green with fright, grip the seat until I shred the upholstery, and lose my lunch in those little brown bags.

I will mail you this note from Villa Cisneros as I think it has the distinction of being the bleakest place on earth. We will stop here for about an hour. It is a Spanish penal colony halfway between Tangier and Dakar, and there is nothing here but the prison and the airstrip. Planes only stop occasionally for refueling. A harsh, scorching wind blows continuously. Everything is the same color—a dusty dun—the adobe buildings, the people, the ground and even one old camel. The prisoners wander around with apparent freedom. And why not? The Sahara is on one side and the Atlantic is on the other and there is no transport, except one camel who looks retired.

We were served refreshments in a small building beside the airstrip—beer only. The custodian looked surprised at the reluctance of the mamas to serve this scarce and delectable treat to the kiddies. I know the inhabitants are looking furtively at our transport and I will be glad to be airborne. I have just vowed never to feel sorry for myself again if I get away from this sad place.

Love, Mama

Dear Lolly and Suzy,

At last we are in Freetown, the capital of **Sierra Leone**. Since the town is nestled in mountains, the airport is across the harbor. As we came across the bay in the launch, the view of green mountains shrouded in white mists reminded me of Hawaii. In the fifteenth century the Portuguese named the country Sierra Leone either because the mountains are shaped like a crouching lion or because during severe storms the mountains roar like a lion. People are still arguing about which reason is correct. There have never been many lions in the country so it can't have been named after them.

Your father came a hundred and seventy miles out of the bush to meet us and take us to the company house, a large, walled, concrete building divided into three flats. The Spencers occupy one and two English families from the Freetown office live in the others. Bob says there is no room for us in the mining camp yet, so we will live in Freetown for some time.

Our flat is nicer here than the one we had in England. We have an electric stove and a fridge, but we still have the same frustrating English wiring. I bought a new iron and rushed home to use it and found no plug on the end of the cord. When one buys an appliance, a plug must be put on to fit the kind of outlet in your house. There are five kinds of outlets in this house. Plugs are round, square or triangular; they are walnut sized, lemon sized or orange sized and three pronged, two pronged, round pronged or square pronged. This means that once you match a plug on your iron or radio or fridge to a wall outlet, you are more or less doomed to keep the appliance in the same place. I like to iron all over the house or to make toast on the verandah so this is a very onerous restriction for me.

I must stop and wash my leeks and chicory for dinner. Chicory is a delicious greens like Chinese cabbage. I thought it was something one put in coffee. A ship came in today bringing these goodies from England.

Love, Mama

Dear Lolly and Suzy,

Bob has gone back to the bush but has promised to visit us as often as possible.

We have a beautiful view from our house of mountains, town and sea. Guavas, limes, oranges, pineapples, coconuts, bananas and breadfruit all grow within sight. In spite of the African's indolence, he is surrounded by a beautiful garden. Frangipani, crotons, bougainvillaea, and allamanda clothe all the ingenious little houses made of packing cases, scraps of tin and Texaco signs. Lilies, philodendron and many kinds of caladiums grow wild along every path. The garden boy laughs when I dig these up and plant them inside our garden.

The house, garden and servants' quarters are all enclosed by a high wall, and the windows are steel casements with heavy burglar bars set in concrete. It is most disconcerting when you want to stick your head out the window. Everything is heavily barred because everyone (I have been told) is a potential thief. I was appalled at this cynical appraisal of Freetonians until I had two pocketbooks stolen. The chief topic of conversation among Europeans is, "How and what was stolen from you since last we met?" Thieves reach through the bars of the windows (only in the United States do houses have screens) with a hook and pull out your bedclothes,

27

trousers or anything that will squeeze through. One acquaint-ance has just had his living-room curtains pulled out and snipped off. Another was sitting in a comfortable chair enjoy-ing an after-dinner reverie when, through one half-opened eye, he thought he saw his hall carpet disappearing slowly out the door. Before he could get on his shoes and give chase it was too late. Even the windsock at the airport is stolen regularly for the small bit of cloth in it. It will be hard for me to become acclimated to this because I hate locks and keys. I have never locked a door in my life.

I haven't learned to shop in the local markets yet, so most of our food is canned. Many Europeans never eat the local food but, being a country girl, I must have fresh food. I send the cook out to forage so we can have a little variety in our diet. I don't recognize any of the greens he brings, so I suspect that he often pockets my three-pence and picks things at random along the path. So far, we have suffered no ill effects and the greens taste delicious. I look out the window and drool when I see the cook's wife, bare from the waist up, stirring her little black pot of okra, tomatoes and peppers. She looks in the house and drools at my packet of sugar and tin of margarine.

We can buy instant coffee here but I am getting used to the strong African kind. West Africa grows excellent coffee and they export a lot of it to the United States. We have a coffee tree in the garden.

We will all get fat in Sierra Leone. One's cook inexorably turns out three meals a day, and it is impossible to escape them. There is great agitation and misunderstanding if I refuse to eat, so the simplest thing to do is carry on. Africans are usually hungry and they cannot understand anyone ab-staining from food voluntarily. Fat is a status symbol and prominent people are generally very plump.

John couldn't agree more with this way of life. His favorite reading has always been the cookbook. He reads Betty

Crocker's copiously illustrated book to the cook, shows him the pictures and orders same. The cook may not be able to read but he can *look* and cook, and if I am not alert we are likely to have lemon meringue pie for lunch, jam tarts for tea and cherry pie for dinner, all with pastry made of pure butter.

The rainy season is on, and such rains—hard, vicious, gully-washers—I have never seen. In some places in Sierra Leone it rains over two hundred inches a year as compared with fifty inches a year in Florida. Along every road are uncovered drains, two feet wide and several feet deep. They are a menace even in the dry season. Drunks and children are always falling in. Our company lawyer from the States, a sober, correct gentleman, stepped backward to get a better angle for a picture he was taking and disappeared for a few minutes down a drain. Now the servants of the house where he stayed refer to him as "na dronk white man."

The rains affect every phase of living. Envelopes have no glue on them, else they would stick together before you could use them. Candy, cigarettes, cookies and film all come sealed in tins. The doors in the house are beginning to swell and stick, opening only when I back into them with a hard thrust of my rump. I found a carpenter's plane in the tool chest and was busily planing off doors and drawers when my neighbor came by and stopped me. In the dry season when the harmattan wind blows down from the Sahara, everything gets so dry that large cracks are left in the doors and the furniture falls apart.

Love, Mama

Dear Lolly and Suzy,

Your father has assembled a small library for me and in my spare time I am supposed to learn and to teach the family all about Africa. I have started out by reading a moth-eaten history published in 1871. Freetown was founded by the British in 1788 as a colony for freed slaves from England and America. England granted freedom to any American slave who joined the Tories during the American Revolution. The Negroes were sent to Nova Scotia after the war and were later settled in Freetown. Other early settlers came from slave ships which the British Navy captured along the coast of West Africa. Still others were made up of West Indian troops who had served in the British Army. Another interesting contingent of early citizens was made up of a group of prostitutes deported from London.

Liberia, which adjoins Sierra Leone in the south, also began as a colony for freed slaves. A private organization founded in 1817 in the southern United States sponsored a scheme of emigration there for freed Negroes. In 1847 Liberia became the first Negro republic. In the nineteenth century Freetown and Monrovia, the capital of Liberia, were two small spots of light on the Dark Continent which were always in conflict with the tribes of the interior. They fought the slave trade tooth and nail, whereas the tribes of the interior found warring and selling captives their most lucrative business. Heretofore, I have always felt terribly guilty about the white man enslaving the innocent black but this is not a complete picture. The black man has always enslaved the black man, selling the victim when an opportunity presented itself. Slavery still exists in Africa today, though usually in such a mild form that it is not recognized as such. In the short time I have been here, I have seen this headline in a Freetown paper: "Man Sentenced to Seven Years for Attempt to Sell Brother." The white man's crime in Africa was putting the slave trade on a mass-production basis.

The descendants of Freetown's original settlers, most of them with English names, are called Creoles. During the nineteenth century they were the educated elite, and many still consider themselves so, but in the political ferment of the present, they have been eclipsed by the people of the interior who far outnumber them. The people of the interior often call the Creoles "Black Englishmen" in derision. I am very fond of the Creoles I have met. They are intelligent, gentle, witty people with a Victorian air about them.

The educated Creole speaks perfect English but the group as a whole speaks Krio, a delightful mixture of all the European and tribal languages. One must be able to speak Krio to make a successful telephone call or to carry on a business transaction. It is the lingua franca of the whole country. Much of it sounds like the patois of Alabama. (Remember that many of the ancestors of the Creoles had been living on the American seaboard a hundred years before they were repatriated to Africa.) As in Alabama, *v*'s are always pronounced *b*'s—seben for seven, shubul for shovel, and nabul for navel. (I was seven years old before I knew that navel was spelled with a *v* instead of a *b*.) Favor, meaning to resemble, and tote are Krio words used just as they are in Alabama.

All of the European languages are represented in Krio. To know is "sabby" from the Portuguese verb *sabir;* child is "pickin" from the Spanish words *pequeño niño;* much is "borku" from the French word *beaucoup* and trouble or talk of trouble is "palaver" from the Portuguese word *palavra.* Palaver is the most useful word in the language. I have

palaver constantly with Krio. "I de cum" means I am going.
I de cum.

Love, Mama

Dear Lolly and Suzy,

If we continue to live in West Africa we should pay off our mortgage at an alarming rate. The advertising man has not penetrated Sierra Leone yet so this is the hardest place in the world to spend money. Only after exhaustive inquiry is one able to find where to buy shoes, thread, nails or rice. Then, once you follow the scent and arrive at the right shop, the clerk will tell you that the long-sought article is "finished." If you persevere, dig around the shelves and turn up the article, the clerk will tell you that you can have only one. Everyone hates to deplete his stock. The shops close for two hours at lunch and at four thirty in the afternoon. If you are in the middle of a transaction at closing time, you will have to wait until the next day to complete it. This vast, silent, insurmountable conspiracy to keep one from buying turns a harmless shopper into a raving maniac. And yet, the town is full of traders, aged from six to sixty, hawking their wares from baskets on their heads. In the baskets are matches, onions, small tins of milk, shoelaces and cigarettes to be sold one at a time. Often the items are sold a fraction cheaper than they can be bought in the shops. Bob says that cash is the answer to this mystery. The market mammy buys something on credit which will sell quickly, then she lends out the cash for a fabulous interest or uses it to deal in local produce. She makes enough money to pay back her debt and have a profit left over. The mammies have good credit with the commercial firms and are a power behind West African commerce. They have fleets of children selling for them. The pickins are sharp and diligent else they suffer harsh reprisals.

Perhaps if I had an unlimited amount of time and patience as the Africans have I would be able to buy everything I want. Everyone is busy trading with everyone else. The big European companies who bring in the goods sell them to the Syrian traders who sell them to the African traders who sell them to each other. Nobody sells them to me.

I found it almost as hard to buy things in London. It is against the law for shops to be open more than a certain number of hours a week and at certain hours of the day. If I want a loaf of bread at 2:00 A.M. in Florida I can always find it but in London I often went without bread on Wednesday afternoon because I forgot it was early closing day. Americans have an ingrained admiration for overabundance but the economy of the rest of the world seems to be based on the theory of not-quite-enough-to-go-around. I suppose it is because nowhere except in the United States is there a market of one hundred eighty million people, speaking the same language and buying the same kind of goods. Our manufacturers can make things cheap and easy because they make so many. Our merchants can afford to stock size eight or size forty-eight dresses, triple-A-cup or D-cup brassieres or pink or blue refrigerators. Oh, I must stop thinking of that consumer's paradise where everyone is insolvent.

Love, Mama

Dear Lolly and Suzy,

The children are getting bored with the rain and town and are eager to push on to the bush and join their father. They have no playmates here except an innocent little girl upstairs whom they torture. Today I heard her screaming in terror and I looked out the window to see Tom chasing her with the skeleton of a dog's head. He fitted his hand into the skull and was in close pursuit of his quarry, chomping the vicious teeth at the nape of her neck. Her mother just managed to save her life by snatching her in the door. They have been cool to us all this afternoon.

It is trying to live in an apartment so close to other people. John, Tom and Rob are the sweetest little boys on earth, but casual acquaintances don't appreciate their hidden virtues. They just wonder why they are not in reform school. How I wish you were here to look after them. The days are gone when I had knee chillun, lap chillun and yard chillun. Rob has now turned into yard chillun and I am hard pressed to keep up.

During the rains I have found time for the gentler household arts and I have been crocheting. As the boys have exhausted all forms of indoor entertainment they, too, have become interested in sewing. It gives one pause to see these wild mavericks sitting in the parlor doing fancy work. Tom turns out foot after foot of grimy chain stitch, wielding the crochet hook like a spear, his eyes a-squint and his tongue sticking out between his teeth. He is content with the pure beauty of the chain stitch but John's creativeness has taken a more practical turn. He is making mongoose clothes.

Mongooses (not mongeese) grow wild in Sierra Leone, and Bob brought us one from the bush. Once you get over your

34

initial revulsion at his ratlike appearance, the mongoose makes the sweetest, most affectionate pet who is crazy about people, even Americans. Mongooses are supposed to be the natural enemy of snakes, so we will take him to the bush with us. He is fearless of everything, chasing dogs, cats and goats. His name is "Weetie" as this is the sound he makes with many variations. He can sound like a bird, a squirrel, a cricket or a chicken.

I have adopted a new little brother for you named Tommy Kamara. He is a Moslem Mende, black as night and about the size of Rob although he is two years older. His father, our houseboy, said he couldn't afford to send him to school, so I have taken on the cost of his education—about fifteen cents a month.

Lolly, it is indecent for you to have fun and make good grades too. What weight can my maternal lectures on the grasshopper-and-ant theme carry when you continue to make good grades? I am afraid you don't get enough sleep. You will have bags under your eyes and sniffling colds if you don't get enough rest.

Love, Mama

FREETOWN<br>JULY 4

Dear Lolly and Suzy,

We have just celebrated a quiet Fourth of July. I felt that I must make some patriotic effort in behalf of these little displaced persons, so I had them sing "The Star Spangled Banner" and we bravely had iced tea for lunch in defiance of the Union Jack which flies over Freetown.

It is really too cold for iced tea. Africa is not so warm after all. This is the coldest July I have ever spent. Although we are

35

as close to the Equator as Panama, we have to wear sweaters at night during the rainy season. I have been reading with nostalgia about the heat wave in the States.

Our English newspapers are weeks old when we get them, but old news is as good as fresh news. Really it is better. Reading about a crisis that is weeks old isn't very damaging to the circulatory system. Out here we read only the good English papers, but when we were in London we read them all. The English press was shocking to me. I was always looking over my shoulder with a guilty feeling that someone would see me reading *The News of the World*. I always bought the Sunday *Observer* to cover it with.

The writing of the English press about America is anything but warm, Americans being depicted as greedy, uncouth, materialistic, stuffed with dollars and tranquilizers. I surely wish I had some dollars and tranquilizers. I have never seen any of the latter and very few of the former.

I am afraid we will need tranquilizers here as we never get any rest. I always thought primitive people went to bed when it got dark (we did in Alabama) but there is varied and frenzied activity in Freetown all night. We live in the middle of Wilberforce Village, a suburb full of people, dogs, cats and goats. The villagers stay up all night, singing, drumming, dancing, fighting or visiting. Our servants who live behind the house have a hand-wound gramophone and *one* record, whose longevity is incredible. I have heard it so often that I will be able to sing it when I get home, provided your grandma isn't listening. It is called "Back to Back and Belly to Belly."

Our flat is on the ground floor of the house and there is no front yard, so hundreds of people stroll by day and night and stare at us through the burglar bars. One is never alone in Africa. When it begins to get quiet about 3:00 A.M., the watchman awakes, stamps his feet and sings to assure us that he is awake. Every house has a watchman, though not one of them has ever been known to catch a thief. It is rumored that all watchmen are in the pay of the powerful burglars' fraternity and when it is your turn to be "teefed," they give all possible aid to the fraternity.

Our watchman is a small, wizened, coal-black man who wears the cast-off army clothing of the world. Along with his British, French and African garments, he wears a GI overcoat, green with age. During World War II several hundred Americans came to Freetown to build a radio station before the invasion of North Africa. The Africans, and Europeans too, proudly reminisce on those glorious days when the town was filled with soldiers and sailors, Free French and Vichy French, spies and counterspies. Freetown's large natural harbor could accommodate hundreds of ships, and many convoys assembled here. Outside our garden wall, overlooking the harbor, is a big, concrete gun emplacement, now fallen heir to John and Tom and the lizards. German submarines used to wait offshore for the convoys and the iron-ore carriers. The mines of Sierra Leone supplied forty percent of Britain's iron when the Germans took over the Swedish supplies.

Graham Greene wrote *The Heart of the Matter* in Freetown during the war. You must read it, if only for his description of the only hotel in town. It is a filthy, vermin-infested, beloved West African institution. There are men sitting morosely on the barstools, pickled in alcohol, who may have been there for forty years. The owner is reputed to have the warmest heart in the world and has never turned away a derelict.

Suzy, I can't remember where I put the insurance policy on the car. Could it be in Florida, Gambia, London or Alabama? When I live in one place, lost things always turn up but I will have to improve my filing methods if I keep moving.

Love, Mama

Dear Lolly and Suzy,

This has been a terrible week. We got the pictures of you and all of us went into a decline from homesickness. Besides that we have had one minor disaster after another.

Today we got a grub out of Rob's head. I felt a bump on his scalp and my neighbor told me it was probably a tumbo-fly larva. I covered it with Vaseline and when the grub came up for air, I plucked him off. It was nauseating and I washed and washed my hands like Lady Macbeth. An English girl told me that she once had fourteen on her bottom. This is because the Africans lay your clothes on the ground or over a bush to dry and the fly eggs get on them. It takes a year of indoctrination to get an African to use a clothes line and I don't think he can ever be taught to use clothes pins. I have talked myself purple but my boy always pins the pins carefully on the line, then lays the clothes on top of them.

This afternoon the cook told me that he had "belly palaver" and I sent him to the doctor with the office manager. He was found to have gonorrhea so the manager sacked (English for fired) him. It's a pity as he was such a good cook. Another of the servants has been drinking palm wine and beating his children. Fresh palm wine is an innocuous, mildly intoxicating brew but when it get older it turns into wood alcohol and makes the drinker blind and crazy. From the sounds going on in the back yard, this wine was very old.

Rob just brought in a present that shook me further. It looked like a pretty seashell the size of a coconut but when he put it in my hands I saw that it contained a huge, pulsating, slimy snail. When I screamed and threw it out, the houseboy rescued it for his supper and said, "Eeeeee—sweet chop, Madam."

38

Rob was hurt that I rejected his present and I have already spanked him once today. He has been slipping money from my purse and buying candy at the African shop up the road. His ignorance of the currency is his undoing. If he is lucky he fishes out only a penny and buys two pieces of candy which can be eaten before he is caught. But if he is unlucky enough to get a two-shilling piece which looks like a penny, he gets forty-eight pieces which he finds it impossible to dispose of before he is apprehended. He carries on his business transactions in silence, holding out his money with one hand and waiting for the loot with the other. He hates getting forty-eight pieces of candy instead of two but he hasn't been able to figure out a solution.

Bob came down to spend last weekend with us and he gave some bush ladies a ride into Freetown. One of them held on to his bare leg throughout the whole trip and he arrived pale and shaken. He didn't know whether she was frightened of the vehicle or just liked his shapely leg. A hundred eighty miles is a long way to hold on to a leg for whatever reason.

The worst of the week's disasters happened when Bob was on the way back to camp. He lost all of my jewels, my opal necklace from Australia, my star sapphire from Siam, my topazes and amethysts from Brazil. Because I am so careless with my belongings, he decided to take the jewelry and put it in the camp safe. He put it in his briefcase on the front seat of the Land Rover but the African driver put it in the back where it bounced out somewhere between Freetown and the mining camp. They came back making inquiries at every village on the way but to no avail. We have offered a reward and the briefcase had our name and address on it but no one has any hope that it will be recovered. I felt so sorry for Bob that I could have wept. The jewelry represented a history of his travels. There is one good thing about losing it. Just think of the tales I can tell my grandchildren about losing the family jewels in the wilds of Africa during the summer of '57. The gems can grow in the telling just like the family silver after Appomattox. Rubies, diamonds, emeralds!

My French neighbor invited us over for tea to cheer me up and I was further depressed to find that her cook spoke three languages, French, English and Susu. He had to interpret for us. I am determined to learn another language even if it is only Mende, the language spoken by the tribe at the mining camp. I have so much to learn.

Love, Mama

OUR NEW HOME
KABATI, IMPERRI CHIEFDOM

Dear Lolly and Suzy,

We arose early yesterday, packed the children, mongoose and cat into the Land Rover and departed Freetown for Gbangbama (pronounced Bang Bama), the site of the mining camp. We found the cat starving in a goat shed, so we took him in and gave him a typical English name, Featherstonehough (pronounced foon).

It took several hours to get out of Freetown as all the gasoline was "finished." One does not start a journey without a full tank and an extra five-gallon can, because outside the capital, there are only three filling stations in the country. We went around town, casually inquiring about petrol. To be hurried and come directly to the point is considered gauche. Finally we got enough gasoline and were off down the Bo road. For the first forty miles the road was asphalt, then it became gravel and finally it turned into a laterite track one lane wide. (Near Gbangbama there were no roads at all until our company built them last year.) Ladies along the road were taking advantage of the smooth expanse of asphalt to dry their rice before husking it. This is the only asphalt road in the country yet the

40

ladies are bold enough to take it over. When a car comes by they scurry around like jealous hens keeping the invader from their piles of rice. They leave just enough room for one vehicle to pass. The traffic consists almost exclusively of mammy wagons, large, three-ton trucks that carry mammies and their produce to market. These lorries are an astonishing sight, bulging with people, petrol drums, firewood, sacks of palm nuts, bundles of piassava, bunches of bananas and strings of live chickens hanging by their legs. The drivers, who are not the owners, drive as fast as the vehicle will run and at every dangerous curve or bridge one sees the hulk of a new lorry smashed by the roadway. They all have whimsical names painted across the front, "Praise God," "Blue Streak No. One," "I'll Always Remember Tomorrow," "Save Me Oh God" and "Friends Today, Enemies Tomorrow." On every hill boulders lie in the road marking the spot where overloaded vehicles have paused for repairs, using stones to block their wheels. When the repairs are completed, off they go, leaving the stones in the middle of the road. Sierra Leone drivers have never realized that a highway is a two-way proposition. They not only use the middle of the road for driving and making repairs but for loading and unloading passengers and cargo.

The scenery along the road is unspoiled by signs except for a few near Freetown advertising Coca-Cola, Sloan's Liniment, Gripe Water and Lung Tonic. I was so happy to see the Sloan's Liniment sign. When I was a child we always had a bottle of that in the barn to rub the mules' legs. Signboards are not very successful in Sierra Leone, because the citizens take them down to build houses. The highway is marked with English signs that say, KEEP OFF THE VERGE, DUAL CARRIAGE-WAY, DEAD SLOW, FILTER LEFT and HALT!

Every village is built on a stream and every stream was full of naked people, bathing, washing clothes, talking politics and

41

airing their differences. They didn't dive for cover but stood up and stared as we went past.

We followed the railway for about eighty miles, a narrow-gauge line of some two hundred miles which has been in the country longer than roads. The average speed of the passenger express is fifteen miles an hour and the chief cargo seems to be gourds full of palm wine brought from up-country to thirsty Freetown. During the war the favorite song of the West African troops was, "De Train fo Bo, She No'Gree for Go." Bo is the chief town of the interior which is served by the train. Bob says the government would dispense with the railroad if they knew how. The deficit caused to the government last year was more than a million pounds, a tremendous amount in this country, one-tenth of the total revenue.

We arrived at Gbangbama in time for a cup of tea. There are four Americans, ten Englishmen and one Canadian living there now but most of them are going home soon and leave only us, I am afraid. The camp has running water, electricity, radios and all kinds of unexpected amenities. But it is really in the bush. For miles before we arrived we saw nothing but a green tunnel of road, lots of grey monkeys and a few half-naked Africans who darted into the bush as we went by.

After tea we drove to our house in Kabati, in the real suburbs, eight miles from the mining camp. There is not room for us at Gbangbama for several months, so we have rented a new house from a prosperous African trader. The house is built of mud and sticks with a tin roof. The tin roof is another status symbol of Africa. The house has six rooms with a breezeway leading to an outside kitchen. The windows have shutters but no glass or screens. It is painted and really a very charming house, much better than the thatched hut I expected. Furniture from camp has been brought over, including a kerosene stove and a big kerosene Electrolux refrigerator.

No white people have ever lived in the village before and

the young children scream in terror at the sight of our pale faces. Think how awful a white face must look the first time you see one.

Bill Siprelle, an American who is doing some consulting work at camp, helped us to get settled and to keep a grip on reality.

Last night I could hardly sleep. Thoughts of snakes and cannibals and leprosy tumbled through my head—and you are so far away. But this morning the bright sun makes everything look different. There is so much to do and so much to learn.

Love, Mama

Dear Lolly and Suzy,

The people in Kabati belong to the Mende tribe, the largest in Sierra Leone. There are twenty tribes, all with a different language. Coming from Freetown we passed through some Temne villages and the natives seem taller and thinner than the Mendes who are squat and muscular looking. All are so black that they look navy blue. The Mendes don't like the Temnes and tell us that they are rascals. The Temnes tell us the same about the Mendes. Having your servants from the same tribe is the only way to have domestic tranquility. The servants for the three apartments in Freetown were Mendes, Susus, Lokos, Mandingoes and Kissys.

Bob is having a fence built around the yard to keep out the goats and people. The whole village has been working on this house for over two years and they have a personal interest in it. The chief comes to look every day with a retinue of wives and relatives. I wonder how long it is going to take for the

43

Mende tribe to see us. I am beginning to think they are importing people from Guinea and Liberia to have a look. Hoards of people come all day, crowding and jostling at the windows for choice vantage spots. Until we got our sanitary facilities working, it was most embarrassing. Behind every bush were several villagers, at least every bush where I sought cover.

Our toilet is a metal can, containing water and a carbolic acid solution, with a conventional toilet seat on the top. Momo, our sanitary engineer, empties it every day in a big pit in the woods. The fact that it is portable confuses me and I can't decide where to put it. I keep moving it from room to room—you know how women like to rearrange furniture.

Bob has breakfast at camp every morning, leaving before we are out of bed. If he forgets to put the board across the opening to the verandah, the goats and chickens come in. You have no idea what a joy it is for a small boy to awake and find a rooster and a billy goat in his room. Rob is going to hate our fence.

I have only one houseboy now and too much work to do. Dozens of people come every day for a job but I want to move slowly when hiring my staff. The boy I have now is as black as night with gleaming white teeth filed to sharp points. (This is done for its cosmetic value—like flat-top haircuts in America.) When I look out the window and catch a glimpse of him in his loincloth, swinging his machete, my heart skips a beat.

Bob has made a fine water system by turning a drain spout into a fifty-gallon drum. For the next few months we will have plenty of rain water and before the dry season we hope to be living in camp. We boil and filter all of our drinking water in a Royal Doulton pottery filter. The Africans do not understand why we boil water. After carefully, with much indoctrination, giving us boiled water to drink, they will refill the ice trays with unboiled water, swarming with amoebas.

44

We have had such fun with the refrigerator. Few of the villagers have ever seen ice and there is no word for it in the Mende language. Passing out ice cubes is our chief source of entertainment. The Mendes' first reaction was like a yearling touching an electric fence but now they love the "hot" water. The children go flying home with the ice as soon as you give it to them so they can show it to as many people as possible before it melts. The chief is too dignified to be seen hopping around with ice cubes, so he sends a servant over with a basket every day to get some for himself.

Suzy, look after your grandma with love and tenderness. If she wants to be crotchety at the age of eighty-five, she has earned that privilege. (Young ladies did go to bed at nine thirty in her day.) When I think of all the troubles she has met and triumphed over, I realize what a weakling I am. Imagine being a widow with nine children. Only five strain my meager ability, even with a father on the scene.

Now that I am finding life a trifle more difficult away from the comforts of civilization, I find a use for Mother's fine teachings every day. As children she taught us that only people who were wicked were afraid. And who in the world wants to confess being wicked? That is why I can tackle snakes and storms and airplane rides and cannibals with the greatest aplomb—at least when I have an audience. That is most of the time, with John, Tom and Rob around.

Another gem of her wisdom which has always held me in good stead was her admonition to be indifferent to food and raiment. She taught us that gluttony was a sin and dangerous to your physical as well as your spiritual being. (This was a clever bit of propaganda for a widow with nine mouths to feed.) Now when I hear people complaining because they can't get this or that, I find that I can always find a substitute or I can do without quite happily.

You are honored to be near such a woman as your grandma.

45

But I *am* aware that aging celebrities can be perverse. She writes me such complimentary letters about you and Lolly, so see that you deserve them.

Love, Mama

Dear Lolly and Suzy,

My kitchen isn't quite complete so a man is working on it today. He digs dirt out of the yard, mixes it with water and throws it with little sharp "plops" into the framework of sticks. The roof was built first to keep the rain from washing the walls away. When the walls are dry they will be washed with a thin coat of cement, but this is done only in expensive houses like ours. The house came right out of the yard and now I have two huge pits beside the house where the earth was dug. They might have found the dirt fifty yards away but that would have meant extra walking. Who minds snakepits in the yard? Besides it makes a convenient place to throw garbage.

The Mendes are fine house-builders. Without nail or board they build cool, dry, substantial houses. The roof is made of thatch supported by large poles tied together with vines, and the walls are of dried mud and sticks. Houses can be round or square. Think of the advantages of a round house—one can never be cornered. We have all of these building materials in Florida, so when I come home for good, I am going to build a Mende house and snap that vicious link between houses and mortgages that plagues poor Americans.

I went inside a native house today for the first time. It contained a hammock, a bed with straw mattress, some stools, chairs and a small, miniature, thatched house. The latter is a

46

shrine where food is offered to ancestors, devils or spirits, whichever one it is expedient to feed at the moment. A few chickens wandered in and out and a small goat was tethered to the bedpost. The earthen floor was clean-swept and the chairs were comfortable. Everything was homemade, the chairs being made from the crotch of a tree, chosen to fit the behind of a man, woman or child. All eating and cooking is done outside, usually only once a day. This house belonged to Madam Bum Titti, a chieftainess who belongs to a prominent family. Bum is a name of distinction in Sierra Leone, like Cabots and Lodges in New England.

Even with their strong scent of urine, the villages are much more pleasing than the average town in civilization. There is none of the offensive clutter of the twentieth century—beer cans, newspapers, signboards, wrecked cars and old refrigerators. Everything in the village blends in a symphony of various shades of brown and green.

We live on the road from Gbangbama to Mattru. Mattru is a large village eight miles away where there is a United Brethren Mission with about fourteen American personnel including a doctor, three nurses, three teachers, a preacher and various wives and children. Nurse Bard, who is connected with the same mission, lives about twenty miles on the other side of Gbangbama. She is from Indiana and has been here over twenty-five years, walking thousands of miles treating yaws, syphilis, malaria, smallpox and sleeping sickness. She has a vast fund of knowledge about Sierra Leone and its ailments, both literal and figurative. Her present protegés (she has had many) are three little orphans called Samuel, David and Philip. They are fat, saucy five-year-olds and when they are bad, she says, "Stop behaving like white children!"

Love, Mama

47

Dear Lolly and Suzy,

We have been starving for fresh food. There is plenty around but nobody sells things. Kabati is so stone ageish that it doesn't even have a market. People "dash" us things but nobody comes around with anything to sell. "Dash" means a present or to give a present. It is a Krio word, derived from Portuguese, I think. Today was a good day for me as I got several dashes—some African spinach, a bunch of bananas and two paw-paws. Paw-paws are papayas.

We never have any fresh meat or eggs. I brought two dozen eggs with me from Freetown which we improvidently ate in a week and I haven't seen an egg since. There are lots of chickens, but Africans don't eat eggs as they are believed to cause sterility. Chickens hatch their eggs into more chickens, small stringy birds with bald heads. Guineas grow wild in Sierra Leone and the chickens look like they have been crossed with the guineas. Chickens are never fed but live on insects and whatever they can forage. Someone has given us a chicken which I have been trying to fatten, but when I throw him a handful of rice he goes squawking off in terror. Nothing but stones have ever been thrown at him, so the minute I raise my arm he is off like a shot. No animals are fed here. Pigs, dogs, cats and the few cows all fend for themselves. The cows are sleek and fat there is so much grass, but rinderpest and sleeping sickness keep the herds from multiplying.

Only once have I had civilized meat in Kabati. It was a prime leg of New Zealand lamb which, I presume, arrived frozen in Freetown. It came up to Bo by the fast express, two hundred miles in twenty-four hours. There a man from camp brought it for me. He proceeded home by foot, by Land Rover and by dugout canoe and when the leg reached me it was "a

48

bit high" as the British say. I covered the smell with garlic, roasted it crisp and brown and we ate every scrap of it.

The villagers eat anything they can catch—rats, lizards, snails, grubs and flying ants. Our fat mongoose and kitten are a sore temptation to them and we make sure they are shut in the house at night. Africans use the word "beef" for any kind of meat, thus a rat is "small beef." The village hunters hunt in parties and use a long, narrow net stretched through the bush into which the game is driven. The net just slows up the prey; then the hunters leap in and club it to death. The usual bag is only snakes, lizards and rats, but if the hunters are lucky they may get a small deer, an antelope or a cutting-grass. A cutting-grass is a giant rat as big as a groundhog. I love his whimsical name. I wonder if he would do for a lawn mower. I have had Europeans tell me that they are good to eat because they are vegetarians and clean. The cutting-grass looks more like a giant mouse than a rat and has a very benign expression.

The main diet of the Mendes is rice and smoked fish cooked with vegetables, palm oil and hot peppers. Often one small fish is put in the pot for fifteen people. It is a good thing that hot peppers are rich in vitamins, because that is the only plentiful nutritious food. All Sierra Leone suffers from malnutrition and undernutrition. This is one of the main reasons for their indolence. The natural defense mechanism for a hungry body is to seek a hammock and rest.

However, Bob says that good nutrition alone would not solve the African's low productivity. He just doesn't like to work. His civilization places no stigma on idleness and no value on work as an end in itself. When I go through the village for a walk, every day seems to be a holiday with the people visiting, gossiping, gambling or sleeping in their hammocks. We people in the States must either work or starve but the bushman has no such unhappy choice. With the palm tree

49

providing thatch for his roof, wine and oil for his table and nuts to sell the European, why worry about work? I sometimes wonder if our Puritan ancestors and the nabobs of the Industrial Revolution haven't sold us a bill of goods. Work, work, work! And for what? Here we are separated by thousands of miles from our sweet daughters and all to buy twin headlamps and teabags in individual slipcovers. No sensible tribesman would ever put himself in such an asinine position. But things are changing; our expensive accoutrements—shoes, sunglasses and bicycles—are being seen and wanted. The book—that Pandora's box—has been opened, and with education the African will become a slave to progress, even as your poor father.

I must run and attend to my school. I continue my classes throughout the summer so the children won't forget any pearls of wisdom. It is so hard to have school with no privacy. People come from the village and stare in at John and Tom, and John and Tom stare out the windows at them. The staring is mutually agreeable and I am the only one who worries about the neglect of Alice and Jerry.

Love, Mama

KABATI
AUGUST

Dear Lolly and Suzy,

I am having the village goldsmith make some charms for your silver bracelet. Bob has a lump of silver that a resourceful young chemist distilled out of the laboratory's supply of silver nitrate. This lump was found among his abandoned effects after he went home. The goldsmith does beautiful work with no modern tools. He uses the fine silicate of a cuttlefish shell for his mold. John, Tom and Rob squat around his fire and pump his bellows for him. They are always in the village watching something being manufactured. Thread is made and cloth woven out of the local cotton. Cotton grows in two colors in Sierra Leone, white and beige. The villagers make their own baskets, brooms, fishnets and even their own guns out of scrap metal and pipe which they pinch from the Europeans. You can always tell the chief hunter in a village because he has a home-made gun and usually has an eye, arm or leg missing.

The machete is the Africans' chief tool and they use it for hunting, farming and house building. The villagers borrow our shovel to bury people. I don't know what they did before we came.

John has learned to make good string out of plant fibers. It is a good thing because there is no place to buy a piece of string if you need one. The content of our wastebasket are very meager as we conserve paper, string, and cardboard. Even so, it is a treasure house for the village children who haul every-thing home, especially the tin cans which the whole town is using for drinking cups. The houseboy gets the things of real value—such as old razor blades—which he sells in the village. It is a problem to throw away really useless things. Used Band-Aids, bottles of pills without labels and personal letters will turn up in the village unless I sneak out and burn or bury them. The houseboy cannot be trusted to destroy anything except my best dishes.

Love, Mama

Dear Lolly and Suzy,

We have just returned from the morning service of the Kabati United Brethren Church, a little thatched house with open sides and an earthen floor. We sang "Sweet Hour of Prayer" and "Softly and Tenderly Jesus Is Calling" and it made me homesick to hear the old familiar tunes even though they were sung in Mende. The sweetest sound the world over is a familiar tune. Surely the most meddlesome people on earth are those who write new tunes for old songs. They are on the level with people who put jelly centers in chocolates.

The head of the flock in Kabati is Pastor George, a literate Mende gentleman who has been so helpful to us since we arrived. He lives nearby and is our interpreter. Church attendance is small because most of the villagers are pagan.

School is held in the same building as the church and it is poorly attended as well. It is difficult for the townsfolk to find the few shillings for tuition. Moreover, most of them see little attraction in reading, writing and arithmetic. They haven't caught the zeal for education that is raging in Freetown and other cities of Africa. Here the government supports one-half of the school if there are as many as twenty-five pupils, while the mission supports the other half. Kabati is in danger of losing its government support for lack of scholars, so I have given Pastor George a few dollars to corral some more.

Education or lack of it is shocking in this country. Great Britain was the last industrial nation to have compulsory education and, traditionally, they have had no talent for, or little interest in, public education. Consequently they have never encouraged it in Africa until recently. This year Sierra Leone had only a hundred and fifty students who reached the standard of our high-school graduate. In the nineteenth century there was only one school supported by government revenue and it was finally closed as "a waste of public funds." The missions have been the sponsors of education in Africa. Fourah Bay College was opened in Freetown in 1827 by the Church Missionary Society of England, and for a hundred years it supplied most of the educated people of West Africa. It almost died out at the beginning of this century, but now with state aid it has been revitalized and will play a major role in the new Africa which is emerging. A high percentage of its students still come from other countries as Sierra Leone's schools don't supply enough students to fill its college. There seems very little interest in primary schools in Sierra Leone. The teachers are hopeless and the equipment nonexistent. I don't know how they hope to build on such a foundation. As bad as the education situation is in Sierra Leone, it is one of the best in Black Africa. The poorest education systems are in Liberia and Ethiopia, the countries which have been independent the longest. Compared with other African countries Sierra Leone has a large percentage of educated leaders, doctors, lawyers and civil servants.

The missionaries have translated most of the tribal languages for their churches and schools. I have a copy of a Mende grammar and, compared to English, the language is very impoverished. There are no words for colors and no word for one-half. The grammar may lack variety but it makes up for it in dynamism. There are no wishy-washy phrases like "La plume de ma tante." I will quote from a list of conversational phrases: "This house leaks. This fish is rotten. Share the meat, Momo. Bring that pot and a cutlass. Catch that animal and kill it. Don't hit it! Cut its throat. I am suffering from gonorrhea. Thatch my house properly."

For counting, the Mendes use their fingers and toes (even as I). Five is a "hand"; ten is "two hands"; twenty is called a "man" (hands and feet); and forty is "two men." The white

man has given the Mende a useful word for many things—
"hondo" (hundred).

Sierra Leone has never taken a census and it would be a mon-
umental task. The government is beginning to make plans for
it several years hence. The concept of counting so many people will be staggering to the average man. How can you get
them to stay at home on census day, and how convince them
that the government doesn't have some sinister purpose in
such a count?

I must stop writing and clean house. To my dismay I am
having a guest for a week. She is an English girl who is coming out to marry one of the fellows at camp. He has found a
house for them in Mattru but wants the girl to stay with me
for a week to become oriented to West Africa. That would
take years rather than a week. I don't know what I will do
with her as I am so busy getting settled and teaching school.
I understand she has been teaching retarded children, so I
will turn John and Tom over to her.

Love, Mama

Dear Lolly and Suzy,

The girl arrived at dusk yesterday as all the jungle noises
were coming into full sound and huge moths had begun to
converge on the Aladdin lamp. She ate no dinner and appeared numb with fright. Rob cheerfully explained that the
drums in the village were pounding because someone had died
in the afternoon. With the light of morning she is in better
spirits, but I still wouldn't bet on the wedding which is sched-

uled for next week in Freetown. She may run screaming for the first plane when she gets out of the bush.

I had two attractive visitors today, the village prostitutes. Not realizing their position, I invited them in and was appalled when their true nature began to assert itself. After a few remarks of greeting they began to sway and clap their hands and started to dance. They danced a number that would have made Salome look like a Pilgrim and implored me to join in. They spit out the windows which is acceptable in Kabati society but I now have screens in my windows so it was quite messy. They kept holding my hands and saying they loved me, all the while trying to pull the rings off my fingers. I finally got rid of them by shoving them out the door and saying that I must continue with my teaching. John and Tom were bitterly disappointed at their departure. They like real-life problems to give them a meaningful program in education.

The visitors had hardly gone before the town fathers came to apologize saying the girls were drunk on palm wine or they never would have come.

The girls wore lappas, the native skirt, which is a two-yard length of material wrapped around and tucked in at the waist. They wore bras made of fishnet with no lining. I am used to ladies wearing nothing at all on the top but these looked incredibly daring. Africans adopt European clothing to be fashionable, not to cover up.

Men often wear fashions intended for ladies. Some trading company has imported a shipload of ladies' coats, 1945 vintage, and on cool mornings you can see sturdy bushmen striding along in them with their knobby knees showing. Used-clothing firms from New York export bales of clothes to West Africa—all kinds and sizes—and occasionally an itinerant trader will bring a bale to Kabati. It gives one a shock to come upon a bushman wearing a lady's shift or a small black boy in red leotards.

When I give the cook costume jewelry for his wife he always wears it himself. And he is very fond of brilliant nail polish. Civilized man is the only drab male animal in existence. His ladies have stolen his shine, but not so among Africans.

Love, Mama

Dear Lolly and Suzy,

We have been watching the women walk by on their way to the farms this morning. They are all bare from the waist up and the variety of bosoms makes one wonder at the wizardry of our brassiere manufacturers. With the aid of bones to suppress and foam rubber to exaggerate, they are able to make civilized ladies look more or less alike. After seeing the different shapes offered by nature, I appreciate their tremendous talent.

Our overemphasis of the human bosom in Western society would seem ridiculous to the bushman. To him the mammary glands are strictly functional—sometimes clothed, sometimes not—often they are tweaked playfully as we pull pigtails in our more inhibited society. Frequently when we are walking in the village an old woman will lift a bare hound's ear breast and point it at one of the children. She is asking, "Is this your child?" or "How many children have you?"—an eloquent and poetic way of discussing maternity.

It is true that an occasional African woman can throw her ample bosom over her shoulder and serve lunch to the baby as he rides along tied to her back. African babies nurse until they are two.

The women all have a beautiful trancelike posture from carrying things on their heads. No native likes to have his hands encumbered. Furled umbrellas, beer bottles full of kerosene, buckets of water, sewing machines—everything is carried on the head. I saw a small boy racing down the hill to school in Freetown with a bottle of ink perched on his pate. A man told me that when wheelbarrows were first brought to this country, the laborers would fill them with dirt and hoist them onto their heads. An Englishwoman told me that once when she and her husband were crossing a river on trek, she looked up in horror to see her houseboy leaping from stone to stone across the river, with their six-week-old baby in a bassinet on his head. Yesterday I saw John and Tom walking down the road with a fifteen-foot bamboo pole, one end resting on each head. Like the Africans they have learned to put a soft doughnut of grass under their loads to avoid calluses.

Perhaps it is a matter of survival that the native wants nothing in his hands but his machete. Last week while we were visiting at camp, the houseboy heard a noise at the door and found a six-foot cobra crawling in. He promptly cut it in two with his machete which was in his hand. Had I gone to the door, I would probably have been carrying a Kleenex. I have so much to learn.

Please write me longer letters. Nothing you do is too trivial to interest me—what you eat, what you wear, your hair styles, your opinions, your ambitions.

Love, Mama

57

Dear Lolly and Suzy,

Lolly, it is too bad that you are studying parasitology at the same time we are living in Sierra Leone. The worst parasites in the world are found in West Africa but you mustn't worry about us; we are healthy stock and besides we were filled with so much serum before we left the States that parasites are terrified of us.

The commonest affliction of the white man here is malaria, so we all take a daily antimalarial pill. There are several kinds of malaria, some mild and some dangerous. The disease is a fearful killer among Africans, especially children, because it is always aggravated by malnutrition and poor care.

A keen observer walking through Kabati can see enough material to supply nightmares for a lifetime. The worst-looking disease is elephantiasis which is caused by a parasite in the lymph glands. It can make the feet, legs, arms or scrotum swell grotesquely. I read of an operation in Freetown where an infected scrotum weighing more than a hundred pounds was successfully removed. How can a scrotum be *successfully* removed? I guess it was successful from the surgeon's point of view.

Sleeping sickness, which is carried by the tsetse fly, is endemic in this country. There have been a few cases at camp among the laborers. The disease comes on slowly and one gets lazier and lazier and sleepier and sleepier until finally the patient is too sleepy to eat. It can be cured nowadays if caught in time. We see lots of tsetse flies sitting around but they are harmless unless they have just bitten someone with the disease. We swat them immediately with no questions asked.

As hot as it gets and as inviting as the streams and rivers look, we can never go swimming because the water may be polluted with liver flukes. They are little worms that get in your bloodstream and eventually, sometimes years later, set up housekeeping in your liver, lungs, bladder or any place that is warm and human.

The indigenes come to me regularly for medical aid, but Bob forbids me to dispense anything but aspirin and milk of magnesia. He says if anything goes wrong I will be suspected of witchcraft. The African loves purges and Nurse Bard says if he doesn't have at least four evacuations a day, he considers himself constipated.

When a patient from the village comes to see me I urge him to go to the mission hospital but he won't go until he has tried the native medicine. Some of this medicine is quite good and some equally dangerous. They have many good treatments for skin ailments but, on the other hand, lime juice and hot peppers are used for eye infections and a poultice of cow dung for cuts and abrasions.

One kind of white man's medicine which the bushman has unqualified faith in is penicillin shots. He calls them "chooks" which is the native word for thorn. The dramatic success of penicillin in the treatment of yaws and venereal diseases makes the African beg for a chook, whatever his complaint.

When I first came here, I couldn't sleep at night for worrying about all the misery around me. I wanted to rush around and save everyone's life that week. Now, happily or unhappily, I am becoming resigned to the fact that I can't fit our mantle of civilization over Africa. We try to drag the underdeveloped countries along at great trouble and expense to give them the joys of our harassed living. If they want penicillin and roads and bridges, they must learn the cost and work and enslavement to the time clock it takes to get them. We certainly shouldn't try to thrust democracy along with penicillin upon them. The average African understands democracy about as well as I understand the Unified Field Theory. All the emerging African countries need a benevolent despot for their head of state until their education, agriculture and industry can catch up with their independence.

Because of ignorance and superstition it is next to impossible to help the bushman. The World Health Organization has sent tons of dried milk to Sierra Leone but a missionary nurse told me that the mothers are too ignorant or lazy to mix and feed it to the children. I have been feeding a village baby that Nurse Bard said was starving. Although I buy the milk and mix the formula and take it to the baby, the father is too careless to return the bottles so I can refill them. Every day I have to go to the TB-infested hut and get the dirty bottles. About fifteen people live in the house and several have TB. Nurse Bard has told the father to move and take his wife and baby before they are infected but he pays no attention. He is one of Bob's laborers and is comparatively well off.

When I first saw the baby she was three days old and her mother was too ill to nurse her. There was not a single piece of layette in the house because the natives never prepare for a baby until they are sure it will live. I made the baby some sacques from Texaco T-shirts which a friend in Freetown gave me. They are soft and warm and colorful, with "Texaco" printed across the back.

The adult Africans don't look after themselves any better than they look after the children. One of our neighbors was bitten by a snake and the only way we could convince her husband to take her to the hospital was to compare the cost of the treatment with a new wife. He still didn't take her until the next day when she was writhing in agony. Now the doctor tells me that she has a terrible abscess, caused as much from the native medicine as from the snake venom.

I have never heard of the mission hospital turning anyone away but they do make every effort to collect a minimum fee. This is for two reasons. First, the native has little respect for free medicine as the medicine man's treatment comes very high. The second reason is that the mission hospital is so poor. The churches at home pay for the equipment and for the salaries of the doctor and nurses but the hospital must try to make enough to pay for drugs and day-to-day expenses. Of course it never does.

I must stop writing about African problems and get back to Spencer problems. Tom is drawing spacemen on the margin of his workbook and John is under the table watching a praying mantis eat a spider. Oh, I've never had enough sympathy for poor schoolteachers before. The minute your back is turned little boys are——.

Love, Mama

Dear Lolly and Suzy,

Oh, you Americans. Until living in Africa I never knew how intelligent even the stupidest of you are, or maybe how stupid the most intelligent of you are. My opinion changes from time to time. You two must come to Africa. It is beyond my feeble capabilities to describe it. Life is so exciting and so boring: so frustrating and so rewarding: so exhilarating and so depressing. I suppose it is thus everywhere but I have never had time to think of it before. With no committee meetings or car pools I have time to think. It is a shame that I am not better trained for this new pastime. I have decided that Dr. Schweitzer came to Africa to think and to get away from Europeans as much as to help Africans.

I even have time here to watch insects. This country was made for entomologists. Every day I see insects stranger than the day before. There are huge moths and butterflies of every color and design—paisley, geometrical, polka dotted, striped. The prettiest one I have seen is a small one of white satin, overlaid with a small design of gold filigree. I don't mean gold colored; the filigree actually has a metallic gleam.

Last night we found something like a cricket, only one and a half inches long, which made such a deafening noise that we thought our ears would burst before we could get him out of the house. The sensation was painful, like being near a 707 jet when it takes off. This morning I went down to Bob's office and the chief clerk had one tied by the leg to a chair, not as an amazing entomological specimen but because "he make fine chop."

There is a stick insect which is common in Sierra Leone and it looks so much like a twig that it even has artificial thorns on it. One of our friends who has lived in East Africa says that there is a moth there who forms a perfect flower when he alights with a group of his fellows. The moths are hatched in different shades of coral and green so they can form the flower, buds, and stem. This seems unbelievable but insects are millions of years older than people so maybe they are smarter.

We do know that some insect in the warehouse is eating Bob's plastic sample bags. Surely it must have taken termites thousands of years to develop a digestive system to make food out of cellulose, yet here is this sophisticated African bug digesting a plastic so new it is hardly out of the laboratory.

Bob says that nature has everything in balance but I am sure there are too many ants. There are dozens of kinds here, large and small, light and dark, fast and slow, vicious and benevolent. (Tom says the fast ones don't bite.) There are many kinds of ant houses, some in trees and some under-ground. The commonest is the large ten-foot-high anthill. The prettiest ant house is pagoda shaped and about four feet high. It has as many layers as the ants can get on before it is toppled by animals or rain. Every day we see large black ropes of driver ants crossing the road. You can never see the beginning or the end of a column. Nurse Bard says that when they invade one's house the discreet thing to do is leave home and let them go through. In a few hours one can return to find a spotless house, all the other insects killed and eaten and the invaders moved on to greener pastures.

John, Tom and Rob play in the back yard on a big anthill, twelve feet high, made of smooth red clay, excellent for toy-road building. I thought the hill was abandoned but John says not. Every day he has to rebuild some of his roads that the ants have changed in the night. Here the boys and ants are at peace but if they happen to step on a trail of them in the grass they are immediately covered with stinging bites. The emergency treatment is to strip off trousers and howl for Mama. Too many of the bites can be dangerous and newborn chickens, puppies and kittens are often killed by them.

It is pouring rain today. I will be glad when September is over. It is time for you to start to the University again. Choose professors who make you work hard so you won't be wasting your time and money.

Love, Mama

KABATI
SEPTEMBER

Dear Lolly and Suzy,

I just made the boys get rid of a present the hunters gave them, a live, scaly anteater. He looks like an American armadillo, with a long snout and tough scales on his back. When

63

he is frightened (most of the time) he stays rolled up in a tight ball the size of a pumpkin.

I evicted the anteater when I found him under my bed eating out of an anthill. The boys had brought the hill in for him to look for his supper. Now my floor is covered with crumbling anthill and swarming ants.

I am going to take steps about all these darned pets. I caught Rob crawling under his bed with an armful of straw to make a lizard nest. He had thirteen lizard eggs in his pocket which he said he had just seen a "lizard letting out in the garden." The house is full of lizards already, fat ones and thin ones, orange, black, red, blue, white and speckled ones. We never harm them as they are good insect killers. Bob has a monitor lizard living in the roof of his office and it is three feet long. All the laborers want to eat him but your father has grown accustomed to his face and would miss his beady eye peering at him through the crack in the ceiling.

The strangest lizard is the chameleon which looks like a small dragon. His eyes are on the sides of his head and can move independently of each other, one looking forward and up while the other may be looking backward and down. It creates a bizarre effect. He changes color in a matter of seconds to match his background, being brown on a tree trunk, green on the grass or black when angry. The Africans believe chameleons are the messengers of witches and get terribly agitated when Rob picks one up. (So do I since one bit him on the lip.)

Witches are main characters in the chief bush religion, animism. Witches are bad spirits but there are good spirits as well. They inhabit everything—water, trees, animals and land. A man must walk carefully in his every action else he will offend one or the other. Sin to us is ingratitude to a loving father but sin to the Mende is a rash act against powerful, unpredictable, crotchety spirits. The pagan worships his ancestors because it is thought that they can mediate between him and the spirits. It would be impossible for a layman to know what pleases or displeases thousands of spirits, so he calls in an expert when he needs advice. This expert is the medicine man or the witch doctor. He devotes all of his time to the study of how to get along with spirits. He is usually the son of a medicine man so he has inherited a large collection of information and magical properties. For a fee, the medicine man will make you a charm to increase your rice crop, to sicken your enemy or to cure your scabies. A "medicine" can be something you swallow or a little package of secret ingredients to wear around your neck or even an evil spell. It is very wicked to threaten to put a medicine on someone.

The English girl who came out has been married for two weeks now and shows no sign of running away. She told me that being around John, Tom and Rob had been such a help to her in getting used to the bush because she couldn't be afraid of things when three small boys were not. I didn't tell her that small boys were not afraid of the devil himself.

Tomorrow we are going to Mattru to a party which the doctor's wife is giving for the new bride.

Love, Mama

KABATI
SEPTEMBER

Dear Lolly and Suzy,

Your father has built us a fine shower stall in the back yard. He could find only three pieces of tin so one side is exposed, the side facing the road. Our house is surrounded by a thick coffee grove, and he thought I would rather have people peering at me from the open road rather than from concealment in the trees. This is a faulty appraisal of my character. I don't care who peers as long as I can't see them. I usually wait until night to bathe when the only hazard is a night adder lying on the path.

This afternoon we got dressed up and waited on the verandah for a ride to our first party in Sierra Leone. Soon an Englishman from camp came by in a Land Rover, taking several laborers to the hospital for various ailments. John, Tom, Rob and I hopped in and drove to Mattru in a torrent of rain.

There are few bridges in Sierra Leone, the main roads having ferries on cables which are pulled across the streams by hand. Our road has neither bridge nor ferry, and to reach Mattru we must leave the Land Rover and cross the Jong River by dugout canoe. At this time of year the Jong is a wide, deep, raging stream full of whirlpools, logs and floating debris. When the canoe starts across, it is rowed a hundred yards upstream, close to the bank, so that when it gets in the strong current it won't be swept past the landing on the opposite shore. About four boatmen paddle furiously while the passengers squat in the bottom of the wet, muddy canoe which is about four feet wide and twenty-five feet long. It is hollowed out of one huge tree. Each time that I cross the Jong and get in midstream, I have the same reaction that I have at the onset of labor pains—I want to call the whole thing off. But there is no turning back and today was worse than usual because I remembered that it was Friday the thirteenth. One of the boatmen has several fingers missing from the ravages of leprosy, so I never really enjoy the trip.

The guests at the party included the English girl, three American teachers, three African teachers, three American nurses, two American missionaries and several Syrian, African and Lebanese ladies from the town. We all told our names and where we were from, how many children we had and any other pertinent information we cared to divulge. I showed pictures of my charming daughters and everyone made proper

66

exclamations in Mende, Arabic, English and American. I enjoyed the afternoon in spite of my wet, muddy coattail. Luckily I had carried my shoes when crossing the Jong, so they were in a pristine state.

After the party I visited with the English girl. She was upset because she had just discovered an unknown boarder in her house. She and her husband rent a large African house in the middle of town but, having little furniture, they use only two rooms. She was looking in one of the unused rooms with an outside entrance and there she saw a bed with an occupant. This quiet, unobtrusive African gentleman had been living there all the time. He was shocked by her wild, unreasonable behavior when evicting him. Imagine two people wanting a whole house to themselves?

Jusufu, my filed-toothed majordomo, went to Mattru with us to visit his father. This means we will have a hard day's work tomorrow because he always brings us two bushels of coconuts as a present. On coconut day we grind them in the food-chopper and put them in the freezing compartment of the fridge. Then we can have ambrosia for weeks. I know that all good Southern cooks should grate coconut, but after grating about ten, ground coconut looks pretty good.

Bob says I am going to forget how to cook—out of a package, that is. I bake my own bread, mix my own cakes, husk my own rice and, in a pinch, make my own yeast out of palm wine.

Love, Mama

67

Dear Lolly and Suzy,

You always ask me so many questions about your brothers. I wish you were here to answer some of theirs. This morning Rob asked me, "What kind of animals aren't there any like?" Then he wanted to know if tapeworms get about. I said, "About what?," and he said, "About as long as this fence."

Unfortunately, too much of our conversation is about parasites and germs. To make the boys be clean and careful about what they put in their mouths, we give them grim lectures on the importance of hygiene in Africa. Consequently they are very interested in microbes and spend hours conversing about how big is a germ's crumb, or a germ's dog or a germ's virus. Speaking of virus, there is Asian flu at camp. This must be the most modern thing that has ever come to Gbangbama. The epidemic in the States is only a few weeks old. One of the men brought it from Freetown but I hope your father doesn't bring it to Kabati.

I just sent John to the village to try to buy threepence worth of bananas and a penny's worth of hot pepper. He brought back fifteen bananas and a pint of hot peppers. I wanted only two pods. I must get some half-penny coins for these big deals.

The village hunters sold us a leg of venison today. The local deer is about the size of a bird dog when fully grown. A man at camp has one for a pet and it is only as big as a cat. It is so beautiful with its big soft eyes that I hate to think of eating one.

I don't know why the natives don't eat some of the devilish goats. There are hundreds of them but they are never eaten except for ceremonial occasions. Goat horns are used to make a ju-ju par excellence, which is supposed to inflame the passions but this is the only useful purpose served by the beasts. They are always jumping my fences and eating my flowers. It is so frustrating to try to grow flowers here. The woods are full of gorgeous things, but it is incomprehensible to the African that I want to bring them into the yard. A flower has absolutely no meaning to a bushman. To grow any plant except for food is absurd. It upsets the garden boy that I let the grass cover the ground. He wants to scrape it bare and I suppose that would make less cover for snakes.

Today is haircutting day. There was a barber in Freetown but here I have to do all the haircutting. I am so glad the children have blond hair because my mistakes don't show so much. At first everyone's hair was full of shelves, hollows and stair steps, but now I can turn out a pretty smooth cut.

I think we are coming home in time for Christmas. We can make the boys' eyes sparkle by talking of the things we will have when we get home—ice cream, hot dogs, hamburgers, a meal in a restaurant, a head of lettuce, fried chicken, movies, a warm bath in a tub, a telephone!

Congratulate your Aunt Sara on running into the sheriff's car. It is clever to be able to have an accident with flair.

Love, Mama

KABATI<br>OCTOBER

Dear Lolly and Suzy,

Rob has been running round naked in the rain, but he just came in because the garden boy was laughing at him. This seems unreasonable because the local children go stark naked until they are ten or twelve. I believe they laugh at Rob because he is circumcised. Among the Mendes this is not done until one is old enough to join the Poro Society and has been

69

initiated into the full rights of citizenship. They think it is funny for Rob to have the burdens of manhood on his shoulders at the age of four.

Most West African tribes have a secret society equivalent to the Poro Society of the Mende tribe. The societies are like our Free Masonry, having different degrees of membership. The initiates must never divulge the secrets of the society, but their worthiness to keep them is probably more important than the secrets themselves.

Each season the society initiates a new group of boys. The Poro devil dances around the village and after various ceremonies the boys follow him into a particular part of the bush. This is a sacred place where the boys must stay until they emerge as men. No woman must go inside or even near this place. If she suspects that she is even near, she must clap her hands to warn the spirits that she is near. The boys used to stay in the sacred bush for months and go through rigorous contests of endurance while learning proper methods of farming, hunting, fishing and the arts of war. Now the period in the bush is much shorter, often being only a day or two near the larger towns. But around Gbangbama and Kabati, we still take our societies seriously, so the boys spend several weeks in the bush. The women have a similar society called the Bundu.

In general, the British have considered these societies a good thing, but there are other secret societies, condoning ritual murder, which the government has made every effort to stamp out. These societies are called Leopard, Baboon or Alligator societies, depending on which of these skins the murderer wears when attacking his victim. The body must appear to be killed by an animal.

All over West Africa the people believe in charms and fetishes to frighten away evil spirits, to keep birds out of the rice, to improve fishing, to restore virility, to ward off sickness and to vanquish one's enemies. The ritual murders are performed to make the most powerful fetish of all, the Borfima or "medicine bag." The society kills a human being to obtain the ingredients. Different societies have different recipes for their charms. I got a recipe from a British government report of a Leopard Society murder trial which contained the blood of a cock, a few grains of rice, the white of an egg, and finally, the blood, fat and spleen of a human body. This is all mixed up and chanted over by the witch doctor and then is packaged for the society members.

The possession of this great and fear-inspiring fetish is supposed to give health, wealth and power. When the society members feel that the power of the fetish is waning, it must be restored by fresh human blood and fat. The main purpose of the societies is, and always has been, to hold political power. The societies are composed of a small and exclusive group and in all the official trials for ritual murder, the accused have been prominent members of the tribe. When a member is called upon to furnish a victim, he does so without hesitation, even a member of his family. The victim is usually an insignificant member of the tribe, a poor relation or a child who is living away from his family.

Sometimes the parts of the body not used in the recipe are eaten, but this is only incidental. The main purpose is to make the medicine, and cannibalism is rarely practiced for gastronomic purposes alone as it was in some of the Pacific islands.

Kabati had a reputation as a strong Leopard Society village and the main building at the mining camp in Gbangbama was originally built to house a unit of the British Army sent to stamp out cannibalism.

Don't worry about us because white blood and fat is not efficacious for ju-jus. Pleasant dreams.

Love, Mama

71

Dear Lolly and Suzy,

John, Tom and Rob have had Asian flu but they are recovering. We have had a very harassing week with one thing and another. Yesterday while Bob and I were having coffee under the good Aladdin lamp, John took a candle into the living room to read and set the draperies on fire. Bob tore them from the window and ran outside while Rob screamed at the top of his voice. Weetie, the mongoose, fishing in troubled waters as usual, jumped up on the table and knocked the butter and sugar dishes off on the concrete floor, making a fine paste of butter, sugar and glass for all of us to run through. Tom was still in bed with flu, almost delirious with fever, but when he heard all the commotion he sat up in bed and began to shout, "I want to say my prayers, I want to say my prayers!"

I don't know why we put up with that devilish mongoose. Twice I have gotten enough eggs from the village to hatch and both times he has found them and broken every one. I had six on the pantry shelf today and I rushed to the rescue when I heard the first ominous plop, but I was too late. Weetie never eats but one egg but he can't resist rolling the others around. He pulls the flowers out of the vases every morning and scatters them over the house. He sleeps in my only hat that I have hidden on top of the wardrobe in a plastic bag. As a snake-killer, he has yet to prove his worth. The only time we ever had a cobra in the house, he was asleep in the rafters. He loves to sleep close to the hot tin roof even though he is already as hot as a radiator. One day when he was asleep in my lap, I put the thermometer under his arm and his temperature was a hundred and four degrees. Mongooses are as hot as frogs are cold. With all their deviltry, they are endearing pets. For years I have sweated to tame the wild things the boys have brought in but Weetie was at home the minute he walked into the house.

Rob has been reading "The Night Before Christmas" to the cook and showing him the pictures. He is very indignant because the cook says the reindeer are bush cows. A bush cow is a local buffalo. The cook won't give an inch and Rob is getting angrier and angrier and shouting in Mende, Krio and English.

Thanks for Tom's birthday cards. They were so big compared to the bobtailed greetings one gets in the bush. There are no new cards to be had, so every one cuts off the old signature and uses them over again. They get smaller and smaller. The thoughtful person devotes great care to putting his signature on an expendable spot.

For our past two family birthday celebrations, we have invited the English bride over and each time the mongoose has made tracks over the cake icing. The girl is beginning to get curious about the design of American birthday cakes, but we haven't confessed yet. We can't throw the icing away because powdered sugar is too hard to come by.

Love, Mama

Dear Lolly and Suzy,

Suzy, I couldn't have been more horrified to hear that you had joined a CLUB, than had I heard you had taken up dope addiction. Indeed, they are the same thing. This goes for Lolly's sorority too. It is all right to look on the sorority as a clean, comfortable boardinghouse but to give it any other virtues is preposterous. These groups are too herdish and time consuming. Think of the reading time spent in those asinine meetings. If you two will make it a point to run to the library every time an extracurricular meeting is called, you will be the best-read students in America. You must learn to think, work and live alone. I have seen too much of group living in Africa. Nobody is responsible for anything and individual initiative is glaringly absent. I don't believe in joining anything except the church, but if joining things is dear to your little hearts, I will not forbid you. You are young and will probably outgrow your enthusiasm for joining. After all, I used to be a card-carrying member of the Daughters of the American Revolution.

I just disappointed some of my friends by refusing to buy a cigarette tin full of rutile. I told him we needed it by the thousand-ton measure rather than the eight-ounce. Unfortunately for ordinary mining companies, the natives associate all mining with the glamor, sudden wealth and corruption that accompany diamond mining.

Bob is accosted in every village by a furtive entrepreneur with a small tin of rich, black rutile for sale. I understand their disappointment when Bob refuses to buy. Diamonds are so much more exciting. I have never gardened or dug in the earth with such enthusiasm. Although even if I found a diamond in my petunia bed, it would be illegal for me to pick it up because mining is so rigidly controlled. Your father is so stuffy that he frowns on my reading his geological books and scratching in gravel beds. I don't want to pick a diamond up; I just want to find one. In 1945 a diamond was found in Sierra Leone which weighed seven hundred and seventy carats.

We went over to Bo to visit a friend who is a buyer for the diamond corporation and he let us see, feel and run our fingers through sacks of diamonds. It is an experience to sap a body's honesty. They keep them in little brown money bags. Rob sat at a table arranging them in little piles of green, yellow and real-colored ones. A few of them are beautiful in their natural state, but most look like small green and yellow pebbles. I probably wouldn't have sense enough to recognize one if I did see it in my petunia bed.

The government does everything possible to discourage diamond smuggling, but thousands of pounds worth of revenue is lost every year through illicit mining. I just read in the paper that the customs men had caught a Belgian at the airport with diamonds taped under his arms. He also had swallowed some which the customs men got with a little patience and a day's wait. Most of the diamonds mined illegally leave the country on the persons of traders who walk across the lightly guarded borders to Guinea or Liberia; then they go to Syria, Lebanon or Israel and finally wind up in the hands of the Russians who are eager buyers of industrial diamonds. Sierra Leone needs every bit of its wealth and it receives nothing for an estimated fifty percent of the diamonds mined. It is easy to mine them illegally as they are not found in deep underground mines but widely scattered in stream beds, on hillsides and even under native houses. Policing this diamond area must be one of the most hopeless jobs on earth.

It is almost dark and I must go and see if the houseboy has filled all my modern conveniences—lamps, stove and fridge all run on kerosene. I have almost stopped the futile habit of slapping the walls for a light switch when I walk into a dark room. Also my sophisticated toe has almost stopped twitching when I think of sewing. I borrowed a friend's sewing machine which operated with a hand wheel and, when I first sat down to sew, my toe always raised itself automatically, seeking the electric pedal. I feel so foolish and always look around to see if the houseboy notices my toe in the air and the stupid look on my face.

I am getting pretty good at sewing with the hand wheel although John as copilot is a great help. I have also mastered the technique of getting clothes clean by beating them on a smooth stone. But I still have so much to learn. I either burn myself or the clothes when I am using my charcoal iron.

Love, Mama

Dear Lolly and Suzy,

I have finally fired Jusufu as I have been threatening to do for weeks. Nothing goes on inside his worthless hide except digestion. Though he is twenty-eight years old, this is his first job and the only thing he likes about employment is payday. He does enjoy being around us and our fascinating paraphernalia. He uses my nail polish and breaks the teeth out of my combs on his wooly head. Every time the Land Rover starts he rushes out and begs to go no matter what stage his work is in. If guests arrive he immediately asks what they brought him even though he has never seen them before.

Yet when I sacked him his surprise was incredible. He wept bitterly, fetching, in turn, the chief, the village elders and Pastor George to intercede for him. So far, I have remained firm. Instead of going back to his home near Mattru, he has moved in with the family across the road and all afternoon I have seen his sad, simian face peering at me through the fence. When I go outside he rushes up and renews his pleas. The only way to end this nerve-racking ordeal is to hire him back, but I won't! I won't!

The final straw leading to his dismissal was his lodging a complaint with the chief against John for stepping on his toe. Africans love litigation and spend most of their time suing their neighbors for real or fancied insults. Their chief concern

76

is compensation rather than punishment for the wrong-doer. This toe incident may have cost us several pounds had the chief not been sympathetic. Imagine poor old John convicted of assault.

The night watchman for one of our drilling crews was fined five pounds in the native court for alienating a man's dog. The European driller was really at fault because he fed the starved dog so much that he spent most of his time with the drilling crew. But the poor watchman had to pay.

The most popular suits between the natives are concerned with petty theft, defamation of character and woman-damage. It is a crime to call someone a bastard or an SOB. Life is so frustrating here that I often think of my associates in those terms, but one must not say them aloud, else you will be hauled into court for defamation of character. The odd thing is that there are so many bastards in the country, you would think they wouldn't mind the name.

Often a husband with several attractive wives will support himself entirely with the money he collects in woman-damage suits. The wives will be instructed to form a liaison with any unwary male, whereupon the husband brings suit and collects a handsome payment from the poor man who has been seduced. The fine for woman-damage in Kabati is two pounds and ten shillings (seven dollars and four cents at the present rate of international exchange).

Our prospecting venture has the only payroll in a radius of fifty miles, so our workers with their regular pay are in ever-present danger of losing time and money in court. In Gbang-bama court is now held on Sundays so the geese who lay the golden eggs will miss as little time as possible from work.

Your father has just come in with a six-valve, battery wireless set! Music out of a box—what next? The garden boy is shinnying up a palm tree to put up the aerial while John, Tom and Rob have run to the village to give out the good word.

77

Yes, we have heard about the Russian satellite. The boys and Bob are delighted but it depresses me—I don't want to fly off into space—Northport, Alabama is my goal. The British are asking us if we have heard of the new American cocktail—half vodka and half sour grapes.

Love, Mama

Dear Lolly and Suzy,

You both have a tendency to identify your friends by the cars they drive. Henceforth, I will appreciate your mentioning their wit, intelligence or charm, if any, rather than their horsepower. From this side of the world, talk of so many vehicles strikes a sour note as the virtue of a vehicle here depends solely on the number of people it can carry.

We went to a football match yesterday between two of our drilling crews. The football they play is really soccer, played in bare feet. About ten minutes before the game was over it started to rain and we decided to leave. Bob started the Land Rover and five of the star players left the field and raced panting after us. Even though the score was one to nothing, team spirit meant nothing when compared with that ten-mile walk back to Kabati. Bob stopped and drove the players back on the field by promising to wait for them. I don't know how they got there in the first place but we took them home. Even in church the aroma of a bushman is something to be reckoned with, but in a car full of sweating athletes, it is overpowering. Bushmen always smell like bonga, which is the dried fish staple of their diet. Africans don't like the smell of Europeans any better than we like theirs. They bathe probably

78

more than Europeans but they don't have the artificial aids of sweet-smelling soap and roll-on deodorants.

When we first came to Africa, I wanted to give everyone a ride but after being imposed on so mercilessly, I rarely offer anyone a lift now. An African will ask for a lift and you say, "Of course, pick you up at eight o'clock." When you go by at eight o'clock, he is lounging in his hammock. He slowly bestirs himself and begins to assemble his paraphernalia: two wives, a goat, a basket of bonga, three chickens and a small boy to tote his umbrella. Even though the Land Rover is already full of passengers, he is not discouraged and manages to stow all his gear inside. In the meantime, Bob is thinking of all the ninety jobs waiting for him that Africans should have done in the first place and he gets madder and madder and his blood pressure goes higher and higher. (Yankees should disconnect the time mechanism in their brain when they come to West Africa.) Nobody has ever yet asked for a ride who didn't keep us waiting.

In the process of packing for our trip home in December, I threw away my Sears catalog. Now I am beset by villagers bearing the catalog and pointing out the merchandise they want me to bring back from America. One wants a saddle (there are no horses here), another wants an electric guitar (there is no electricity), and Madam Kabati wants a pink slip and high-heeled shoes made of narrow straps. She is undeterred by the fact that the slip is made to fit sylphlike figures rather than her stately two hundred and fifty pound shape.

Madam Kabati is my best friend here even though she has fallen into disrepute among the missionaries for having taken on a Moslem husband and his religion. She was educated at the Christian mission and speaks fluent English. She is probably unaware that her position as chieftainess would have been impossible had she been born in the Moslem faith. The Moslem faith is growing in Africa because the Moslem mis-

79

sionaries are black men and the religion allows polygamy. Another disadvantage of the Christian missions is that the African doesn't understand all the different sects of Christianity.

However, I don't see how the lowly status of Moslem women can be reconciled with the high status of West African women. Perhaps this will tend to slow the growth of Islam. In spite of the fact that the Mende lady does most of the work around the house and farm, she holds a dignified place in society and can even become a paramount chief.

Misses Spencer, forgive my waspish remarks about what you write in your letters. To get a letter from you, I would willingly hear of the color, chassis and horsepower of every vehicle belonging to every young blade in America.

Love, Mama

Dear Lolly and Suzy,

We had four guests from camp for dinner last night. As we sat down to eat we heard an excited crowd coming up the road from the village. They brought in one of the hunters with blood gushing from his arm and great scratches across his back. He had been attacked by a leopard while inspecting his traps (snares which catch the prey by the legs). The hunter thought the trap was empty and walked too close to it and the leopard mauled and bit him.

Bob took the man to the hospital in Mattru and we continued the dinner party without him. I thought our guests (two were big strong Americans) would go and catch the critter, but no one wanted anything to do with an angry leopard at night. Today the hunters went back to the trap, but the animal had gnawed its way out. Rob will stay on his side of the fence today because leopards are nasty under the best of circumstances, much less when they have been provoked.

Since we have the only vehicle in eight miles, Africans are always coming to us in distress. Every weekend that we have been here, Bob has taken someone to Mattru to the hospital. Last week a man fell sixty feet out of a palm tree and broke his back. He was carried eight miles here by hammock, loaded into the Land Rover and bounced eight more miles to the river where he was ferried across by dugout canoe to Mattru. He survived, although the trip alone was enough to kill him.

When an African is sick or wounded, his friends are so gentle and sympathetic, crooning to him and patting him as we would a child. Yet they are absolutely brutal to animals, kicking and starving their pets and breaking the legs of animals they trap until they are ready to eat them.

The Englishman is just the opposite, being mad about animals but having little time for human beings. He feeds his children at separate meals and sends them away to boarding school as soon as they are out of diapers. But English children are so well behaved—it must pay to repress them.

Lolly, you are much too frivolous for a college sophomore and you must get some serious thoughts into your head. I will give you one—our income tax is twice as high here as in the States.

Love, Mama

Dear Lolly and Suzy,

I visited the hospital in Mattru today and came away with the greatest respect for missionaries. They and absent-minded professors are my favorite kind of people because I love human beings who swim upstream.

The hospital is very poorly equipped, lacking everything but patients. Henceforth I will give serious thought to whatever I contribute to a mission barrel. Articles sent to missionaries should be the newest, best and most durable that it is possible to obtain. Each piece of equipment in a place like this does the work of ten in civilization. I saw an examining table and a machine to make urine analyses which should be in a medical museum, but they are used every day by the Mattru staff. The machine for urine analyses was run by hand like an old-fashioned coffee-grinder.

The doctor is young and enthusiastic and proudly showed me the hospital and discussed his plans for it. There are no catering facilities so each patient brings along a member of his family to cook for him. They have a special place for the cooking and I saw little black pots of rice and vegetables stewing over an open fire.

The doctor speaks Mende but he also has an interpreter who interviews the patients with him. He told me that witchcraft among the Mendes is still very strong and he has had several patients die for no physical reason that he could discover. If a spell or curse is put upon a Mende he will die because he expects to die.

Most of the patients are seriously ill before they are ever brought to the hospital. The staff is very proud if they get a maternity case who comes because she wants to come. Few babies are born in hospitals and the infant mortality rate of

Sierra Leone is at least fifty percent and probably higher. There are no accurate statistics. When a woman has difficult labor, the other ladies come to her aid by pounding on her abdomen. Many babies are brought to the hospital dying of tetanus because the umbilical cord has been cut with a filthy knife.

After our hospital tour we had some creeping eruption frozen on Rob's toe, sipped a glass of iced tea with the nurses and made our way back to Kabati.

This creeping eruption is caused by the same parasite which we have in Florida. Florida also has the same type of hookworm that we have in Gbangbama. You two be careful, living on that dangerous continent.

Love, Mama

Dear Lolly and Suzy,

The children are begging to go to the rice farms with the harvesters today but I must wait until an interpreter comes by so I can tell how far they are going. Some of the farms are as far as seven miles from Kabati. In November the final harvesting is done and early in the mornings the men, women and children stream out of the village toward the farm.

As a would-be farmer and a rabid conservationist, I find the farming methods of Africa too depressing for words. It would be impossible to make poorer use of the land than is made here. The main reason is that it is not individually owned but belongs to the tribe and the chief allocates it to families. There is no incentive for a man to improve his land. Indeed, in some places it is against the native law to do so.

It is forbidden to plant permanent trees lest this prejudice the next allocation of the land. I have wondered why there weren't more mango, coconut and banana trees when they will grow so easily. I have always had a compulsion to plant things and since I have been here I have been berating the poor Mende for his lack of enthusiasm for this activity. Every time a bushman comes near I thrust a seed or a seedling upon him but I doubt if one has ever been planted. Now that I know it is against native law to plant trees indiscriminately, I will let the poor farmers rest in peace. I have so much to learn.

There are no beasts of burden and little farm machinery in Sierra Leone, so the land is cleared by burning. The first thing one notices about the landscape here is the pattern of varied colors, charred brown patches just burned for planting, the pale green of the newly planted crop and the darker green of the patches that have gone back to bush. In spite of the deceptive-looking green growth, the soil in Sierra Leone is poor and should be used for forests instead of farming. The heavy rainfall leaches all the good from the soil. There is no fertilizer so the land must lie fallow for at least four years to grow any crops at all. The period used to be seven years but as the population increases there is less and less time for the land to renew itself. The farms are not square fields as we know in America but just patches full of stumps and logs that failed to burn during the clearing and are too heavy for the farmer to move. How can he dig stumps when his only tools are sharp sticks and the native hoe? Besides if he leaves in the stump and the root system, the bush will grow much faster when he lets the land lie fallow.

The main crop is upland rice. I thought rice grew in paddies and I never heard of hill rice before. In Sierra Leone the rainfall is so heavy that the crop is irrigated from the sky. Swamp rice does grow here along the coast and the tidal rivers. It has a much heavier yield than upland rice but the coastal land is so densely covered with mangrove trees that it takes heavy machinery to clear it. The Agricultural Department has started a program of clearing this land for the farmers which is very encouraging.

The farmer doesn't worry as much about his crops as I do. Especially now that it is harvest time and it will be almost a year until the hungry season comes again. There is drumming and dancing in the village all night at this time of year. There was so much revelry last night that I enquired about the special occasion. The cook said, "No ting, Madam. We jus happy too much."

Many ceremonies accompany the Mendes' rice growing and harvesting. When the rice is planted small soapstone figures are buried in the fields to assure a good harvest. If the harvest is not good the farmer digs up the figure and beats it. When the rice is harvested the first bit is prepared as an offering to the farmer's ancestors. Every respectable pagan household has a little shrine to offer food to ancestors. The food is sure to be gone in the morning because there are so many accommodating ants about.

After the main harvest in November comes the most popular time for marriage. With the larder full, the young men can think of obtaining a wife. It is not easy for an ordinary boy to save enough money to purchase a wife. They must pay from ten to thirty pounds to the girl's family. (A pound is approximately three dollars.) The older, richer men of the community snap up all the more attractive girls because the parents are happy to have their daughters join a prosperous household. The chiefs have many wives because they have the choice of marriageable girls and must pay only a nominal fee to the parents. This, however, is a mixed blessing for the chief because it gives the girl's parents the right to "beg" him when they are in need of help or influence. An Englishwoman told me that she once met an old chief who was literally on starvation because his thirty-two wives and their relatives had eaten him out of house and home.

One of Bob's laborers has never been able to save enough to buy a wife of his own and last month his brother died and left him two. Under native law he is obligated to take his brother's wives and be responsible for them. He told Bob that they were lazy and did nothing but eat. You never saw such a long face over an inheritance.

It is impossible for Europeans to sort out the relationship of Africans. A "brother" can mean a man from the same tribe, or from the same village or from the same father. "Father" can mean uncle, grandparent or parent. One's children belong to the tribe or the family rather than wholly to the parents. Often a child is sent away from his parents for other members of the family to rear.

The children all work like dogs. When you see adults walking along the road, a child is invariably staggering along with the heavy loads on his head. Bob says it is wrong to interfere with this system. The adult has served his sentence of childhood and it would be unfair to deny him the service he is now due.

I must go and put your brothers to work. They have so much to learn.

Love, Mama

KABATI
DECEMBER 1

Dear Lolly and Suzy,

We have been in Africa almost a year. I know that we are supposed to have ten-month tours but your father is too busy to leave just now. We will be home for Christmas even if the boys and I have to come alone.

We were invited to a fete in Gbangbama last night and I met Paramount Chief Kpana Bum for the first time. The chief was pleasantly drunk, lounging in his hammock in his shabby compound, surrounded by crumbling mud walls, two small, upside-down cannons and innumerable wives and children. After paying our respects we went outside where the dancing was in progress. The dancers formed a long black snake of people with an occasional blond Englishman sandwiched between two Mendes. The young fellows from camp participate in the festivities when they are invited. There seemed to be no pattern to the dance until you looked down at the hundreds of pairs of feet, young and old, all moving in perfect rhythm.

In Africa there are dances for every occasion—funerals, weddings, and harvests—and dances for every age and sex. Every African activity is portrayed in dance—cooking, fishing, farming and hunting. In one dance even the victim of yaws is portrayed, hopping on the sides of his feet to show his painful gait. (Yaws makes terrible sores on the feet.)

There are many kinds of drums, small ones made of a single section of bamboo, large ones of a hollow tree trunk and medium ones made of goatskin. To aid the rhythm there is the clap of hands and the rattle of the shake-shake. This is a gourd with pebbles inside.

Whatever the time of night, African children attend all the festivities. We took John, Tom and Rob to keep from offending our hosts and from offending John, Tom and Rob. Rob went to sleep about ten o'clock in the back of the car but the other two held out until past midnight. I missed them once and found them at Kpana Bum's house beating his drums and admiring his collection of leopard skins.

Someone brought me a fat baby to hold with a bottom as bare as my palm. Tied around his waist were dozens of charms to protect him from all disasters. I hoped they would protect me from the bare bottom and they did. African babies are housebroken as soon as kittens. They never wear diapers, so it is very convenient for mama to hold them over the edge of the porch when she notices a restless wiggle.

I have finally discovered, in the absence of pink and blue bootees, how to tell a boy baby from a girl baby—earrings. Mende girl babies have pierced ears and wear earrings from the age of one month.

We thoroughly enjoyed the social life of Gbangbama and look forward to moving to camp when we come back from leave.

Love, Mama

KABATI<br>DECEMBER

Dear Lolly and Suzy,

By the time you get this we will probably be home, but I keep writing because it makes you seem closer to me. Until I went away from you I never knew there was solace to be derived from writing letters as well as receiving them. When I miss you the most I sit down and write furiously. I often wonder if you have time to read all the epistles I bombard you with.

We don't know how to say good-bye to our friends gracefully. If we go away for even a day without telling them all good-bye, they come around and chide us. Africans are the most polite people on earth and I hate to offend them. When we come back we will live in Gbangbama and I can't bear to tell my friends from Kabati that we are leaving for good. I have been dispensing the remains of my hundred-pound bag of sugar to my neighbors for the past few days so they must know that our departure is imminent.

We will come home by Dakar, Lisbon, New York and

Birmingham. Bob will follow in a week or so and we will all be together for Christmas. It is so hard to get started on a trip from West Africa. We drive a hundred and eighty miles over this dusty, rough road; then the following day, after standing on the sizzling wharf for several hours, we take the launch twenty miles across the bay. We then stand in the hot sun for another hour while the bus gets loaded to take us another ten miles to the airport. We stand and wait and wait in customs while they hopefully examine our meager belongings for diamonds, and finally we take a small grasshopper plane to Dakar where we spend the night. The next day we are welcomed into the arms of Pan American Airways who take us all the way to New York. I love those people. They seem so glad to see us, at least for a while.

It will be wonderful to get home and have a mental rest— no rushing streams, angry leopards or plasmodium falciparum to menace the small fry. Their most dangerous adversary will be an irate schoolmarm.

But this tour has been easier than I anticipated. Aside from a few grey hairs, I have not suffered and I have learned so much. Your father's work is going well and he is finding lots of rutile.

When you meet us in Birmingham don't bring any of your friends. We will look like migrant farm workers with our homemade haircuts and our last year's winter clothes. Our clothes have not been cleaned once as there are no dry-cleaning establishments here. The boys have grown slightly, judging from the sweater sleeves up to their elbows. They will be carrying assorted treasures—an eighteen-foot python skin, a scaly anteater hide, a fierce Bundu mask and a homemade Mende pistol.

But we will be solvent, mind you.

Love, Mama

89

# Tour II: 1958-1959

Dear Lolly and Suzy,

We are leaving at four thirty for Lisbon so I will write a
small note while I still have time to put it in this wonderful
U.S. postal system. After living abroad I will never, never,
never complain about the United States mail.

I am so glad we decided to spend two days in New York
because the boys have never stayed in the city proper before.
They are delighted that the hotel has television—and in your
own room, yet. Yesterday in Woolworth's Tom started to make
a ten-cent purchase and John called him aside and whispered,
"Don't pay the first price. Talk to her about it." We have
taught them to never pay the first price asked for anything in
Africa and now, under these futile circumstances, our teaching
comes to fruition.

Last night Bob and I left the children looking at television
and went for a stroll around Times Square. From now on I
will do all my shopping for gifts to take home right here. We
saw replicas of all the junk we have hauled home from India,
Australia and Fiji at a better price than we paid at the source.
I saw a coconut doll exactly like the one I lugged home from
Fiji and I saw some cultured pearls for half the price I paid
in Sydney. I have always known never to buy anything abroad
that is made in the States. Now I know never to buy anything
foreign until it has been exported to the States.

We left our mandolin on the plane from Birmingham to

New York. There was a terrible snowstorm during the flight, and when we arrived I was so happy to be on the ground that I rushed out of the plane, leaving the mandolin and a stack of Alice-and-Jerry books, both of which are irreplaceable in Africa.

I have been thinking about what a peculiar place the United States is. Why don't women ever spend the day at home? I mean *all* day—no shopping, no car pools, no PTA, no church meetings—just stay at home all day. The ladies would love it if they had courage to try. Most of the women I know were on the road, coming or going at least half of every day. If they stayed at home it would solve all the traffic problems and we could stop chewing up all of our beautiful country to make concrete roads. Each time I come home I am shocked to discover more and more people and roads and fewer and fewer trees and meadows.

Another thing that shocked me about civilization was the casual way they shoot, stab and beat people's brains out on television. I see nothing that brutal in Africa. I think letting children watch television indiscriminately is about like letting them smoke marijuana. It helps them get rid of their aggressive impulses etc. etc.

Another thing that upset me about civilization is all the modern writing that deals with abnormal people. My niece was writing a paper on modern playwrights and it made me wonder if you two think that Tennessee Williams' characters are typical of the stream of humanity. He is such a good writer, it is a shame that he is a crackpot. One of the nicest things about Africa is that they never heard of Freud and sex is just one of many things, not the beginning and end of all. I don't see how the civilized world let Freud, that peculiar little dried-up man, sell them such a bill of goods.

The bushman is so refreshingly different from modern literary heroes. He never falls in love with his mother or his

94

sister or his best friend. He falls in love with a *woman* but he never lets it distract him from the important things in life like thatching the roof or planting the rice or striving to be an upright member of his tribe.

We are so happy to have your papa on this trip with us. He usually manages to precede or follow.

Love, Mama

Dear Lolly and Suzy,

We have had a fine week in Portugal in spite of what the Portuguese call "English weather," meaning sleet and rain. The climate must be like Florida's most of the time because there are palm trees down the middle of the wide avenues, shading the beautiful, tiled sidewalks.

This hotel is too American to be exotic. It has heat and air conditioning by Carrier and elevators by Westinghouse. Your father doesn't understand why this makes me vaguely unhappy. We three ladies will have to do a grand tour sometime and leave the men of the family at home.

We rented a car and drove through the countryside where we saw beautiful farms, orange and olive groves, castles on mountaintops and collards six feet tall. The collards are called "cabbage on high legs." I saw two other things that stimulated my interest: people walking barefoot in the sleet and a footbridge sixty feet tall in the middle. The bridge was built over a small river in a perfect half-circle to permit boats to pass under.

We drove to Coimbra, the site of the old university where the students are supposed to wear flat black hats and capes

95

like Mr. Sandeman. It was so rainy that we didn't see any students at all, but we heard the bell in the old bell tower which the students call the "Goat."

Driving back from Coimbra the chauffeur turned on his radio and it played "Dixie," "The Yellow Rose of Texas" and "Swing Low Sweet Chariot." Bob and I thought this was a bizarre accompaniment for seeing old Portugal but the children saw nothing strange about familiar tunes coming from a radio.

We wanted to go to a bullfight but there were none to be seen this time of year. The bull is not killed in Portugal as he is in Spain but is fought until he is exhausted. I finally saw a movie I have been trying to see for years, but by the time I caught up with it the name had been changed to "A Volta ão Mundo em 80 Días."

We fly down to Dakar tomorrow and then to Sierra Leone the next day.

Love, Mama

DAKAR,<br>FRENCH WEST AFRICA

Dear Lolly and Suzy,

Mes enfants are gobbling French food just as though they never heard of chittlins and grits. I expect them to be sick momentarily—Portuguese cuisine for a week, and now French. In Lisbon all the rich food was redolent of olive oil and the waiters plied us with port at every meal. Tom has just disgraced us at this beautiful hotel by biting a semicircle out of a fragile wine glass. It was empty so I don't know why he was gnawing on it.

I met an American girl from the consulate here who just returned from Timbuctoo. She went inland by lorry, seven hundred miles to Bamako, then took a boat down the Niger to Timbuctoo from where she mailed her Christmas cards.

I am writing this on a sunny terrace bordered by geraniums with the Atlantic lapping at the shore a few feet away. A big gameroom adjoins the terrace and yet the boys are whining for something to do. We have been traveling too long. I must get back to the bush and get them in school.

Your father doesn't lack for things to do. The beach is full of bikinis encasing French ladies of all shapes and ages. It is a good thing he has new glasses.

Love, Mama

Dear Lolly and Suzy,

I am settled back in the bush where a white face is a rarity. There are about fifteen hundred Africans to each European in Sierra Leone.

I hear a mournful elephant-tusk horn blowing in the village so the chief must be returning from a jaunt. They always blow this horn to herald the chief's arrival and departure. We are living in the mining camp at Gbangbama now. It is perched on a rocky hillside overlooking the village about a quarter of a mile away. On clear days we can see a spot of ocean glittering through the green jungle twenty miles away. It is very beautiful.

We cook, eat and have our lounge in "the Mess," an old stone building built by the British Army. This building was put up to house an army unit after the hut-tax rebellion in 1898. The Mendes seem so lazy and peaceable now that it is hard to believe they were the chief war-boys during the rebel-

97

lion. Until 1898 only the area around Freetown—the colony—was under the protection and control of England. But in 1898 with the agreement of the chiefs, a protectorate was declared over the whole interior. Naturally this meant that the area must have police and administrative officials and money to pay for them, hence the imposition of a hut tax. The chiefs were outraged and under the leadership of the Poro Society organized the war-boys and tried to drive out the white man. Down with slave suppression, taxes, missionaries and district commissioners! Hundreds of Creole traders and missionaries were killed, several Americans among them. The British Army finally put down the rebellion and hanged thirty-three chiefs. Several were hanged in Gbangbama. The army has long ago departed and "the Mess" was abandoned when our company leased it.

Grouped around the old stone building are eight aluminum prefab houses, each with two spacious, egg-shaped rooms connected by a shower and toilet. There are windows all around the house like the gondola of a dirigible. Someone told me that a retired Zeppelin crewman lives in one of these houses on a hill in Ghana. He has installed fake controls by the windows and sits happily cruising over the world. These aluminum houses are very hot in the daytime but we are comfortable at night because there is a good breeze.

After breakfast each morning John, Tom and I go to school until noon. It is a problem to get rid of Rob. We try to leave him with the cook and the mongoose but he wants to go to school. I hope John and Tom are keeping up with the fourth and second grades in America. My handwriting is so terrible that I never teach them to write. I have them copy exercises from the writing book. I have heard that the American missionaries are starting a school for their children and I hope that we can get John and Tom in that next year. After the fourth grade I won't be able to teach arithmetic. I have my school in one of the little houses that isn't being used so I can get the children away from their toys and the refrigerator.

The boys are happy to be living in camp in the midst of things. Every kind of activity is carried on to some extent, all of it appealing to small boys. There is an electrician, a carpenter, a plumber, a painter, a welder, a chemist, a driller and a mechanic, and on Thursdays when Nurse Bard comes there is a dentist, doctor and nurse, she being all three. There are only four white men including Bob so they switch from role to role as the situation demands. The control of the project has switched from English to Australian, so we will soon have some Australians at Gbangbama.

There are seventy African workers and twelve house servants. With all this domestic staff to manage, I have three times as much work to do as I had in Kabati. The most cruel thing one can do to a housewife is to give her a dozen Mende servants. Each of them does only one kind of work; one cooks, one cleans, one washes clothes, one irons, one totes tea, one washes dishes and one washes pots and pans. There is hell to pay if any of the jobs overlap. Don't-do-anyone-else's-job is the only activity I have ever seen Africans pursue with energy, unanimity and diligence.

Love, Mama

Dear Lolly and Suzy,

Rob is learning to read. All five-year-olds should go to school as they do in England. They are ready to learn and should not be pussyfooting around with finger paints and sandboxes. Rob is such a nuisance when we include him in

99

school but so forlorn when we exclude him that we have started him off reading.

The harmattan wind is blowing this time of year and the air is hazy with dust from the Sahara, a thousand miles away. Everything is covered with a film of dust in the mornings. The haze is not unpleasant as it keeps the sun from being so bright. Early in the morning thick mists rise up from the valleys, outlining the tall palms and mountaintops in sharp relief against the snow-white fog below. We are above the mists and the view is so beautiful that I am happy to be in Africa. Then I go up to the Mess and the frustrations begin. Jenny, the washwoman, has been washing her clothes with ours. She personally may be very fastidious but I can't help thinking of the syphilis, craw-craw and tuberculosis that abound in the village. Jenny is a lean, tall, toothless old crone who makes all the other servants step. She is a leader in the Bundu Society, a veritable dowager of Gbangbama. She is the first woman I have seen working for Europeans which is indicative of her independence. I must not alienate her or she will "witch" me.

One of the Australians has had fifty pounds stolen from his house and we have brought in a witch doctor from Mattru to find the thief. He brought along a "Shaker" who is his assistant in crime detection. The suspects (all the servants) were gathered together and given a handkerchief to hide on one of them while the two detectives retired behind the house. The witch doctor gave a remarkable demonstration of his power by finding the handkerchief the moment he returned. Then he was ready for serious work. He walked up to his Shaker, rubbed his hands under the Shaker's sweaty armpits and touched each of the suspects with the dainty moisture. Then he returned to the Shaker, waved his hands slowly and began to hypnotize him. When the Shaker was completely hypnotized and began to shake like a leaf, the witch doctor gave him a bundle of switches and he started to walk slowly among the suspects. Suddenly he began to beat the garden boy over the head and shoulders and continued to do so until the witch doctor clapped his hands and brought him out of the trance. I would like to make a perfect story and say that the garden boy confessed, but he didn't. We repeated the performance the next day and once again the switches chose the gardener but he never confessed even though the other servants assured us that he was guilty. It was a very eerie ritual, especially when the victim cowered in silence and rolled his eyes while the switches thrashed him until they drew blood. If I had been he, I would have grabbed the switches and beaten the Shaker.

Lolly, stop talking of love and marriage. If you will leave that poor boy alone and let him study, he might make a fine son-in-law some day.

Love, Mama

SULIMA<br>NEAR THE LIBERIAN BORDER

Dear Lolly and Suzy,

Rob, Bob and I have driven down to Sulima to look around before the driller and his crew start to work here. This town used to be a thriving place in the slaving days, but its chief industry now is a small bit of diamond smuggling into Liberia.

We are staying in the United Africa Company rest house, surrounded by abandoned warehouses, crumbling stone foundations and Victorian lampposts. At the beginning of the century this big trading company used to bring its goods in by sea and send them up-country from here via the rivers. But now the mammy wagons and the railroad take the goods up-country from Freetown and all this installation is deserted except for us. The village of Sulima is about a quarter of a mile away, the Moa River is in front of the house and the Atlantic Ocean is on the left.

It seems like the end of the world and I was a little condescending at first until the chief said to me in perfect English, "Oh, you come from Gbangbama? That is a very bad place. When I was a small boy I once went there to see six cannibals hanged." Our chiefdom does have the reputation of being one of the most backward in the country—sort of the Alabama of Sierra Leone. When lorry drivers come up from Freetown on business, they always refuse to spend the night and drive back to civilization no matter how late it is.

The rest house in Sulima is used chiefly by Europeans coming here to fish. It is meagerly furnished by American standards but palatial by bush standards. A rest house is usually one room with a thatched roof and an earthen floor and no furniture. This fine place has a wood stove, two brass bedsteads and a bathtub. No water, of course, but a tub.

The guest book makes better reading than *Confidential*. Visitors are supposed to pay the caretaker three shillings per day and if you don't pay he writes his candid opinion of you when you leave, using faultless English and a beautiful Victorian script. (Sulima is an old mission station and there are many literate people.) I devoured this delightful gossip even though I didn't know the principals. The wit, rancor and scandal were splendid. One British Army captain from Freetown "refused to pay one farthing, used abusive language and his wife left the house in a state of filth." The Spencers paid and left a generous tip for this rascally bush Pepys.

I am looking out the window at your father fishing for tarpon from a dugout canoe with one canoeman. A tarpon will drag that little cockle shell to Bermuda if Bob intercepts one. Many big tarpon are caught here and when one strikes, the canoeman paddles furiously to shore and the fisherman runs up and down the beach playing his catch, until either the tarpon or the fisherman gives up.

Sulima is at the mouth of the Moa River which drains a large part of the diamond area of Sierra Leone. Rob and I have been spending our time sunbathing and sifting sand and gravel by the ton. Just looking, mind you.

Love, Mama

Dear Lolly and Suzy,

It takes fifteen minutes to get a letter started if I want to put the date on it. Finding the date is no mean achievement here where no newspaper or radio reminds you of the date every five minutes. If I happen to know the month, I look at the calendar but then I don't know what week of the month it is. I just called in the houseboys and they told me that yesterday was payday which is once a week. With a little calculation, I have arrived at March 6 but it could be March 13. If I weren't so lazy I could walk down to Bob's office and be sure. I think he cuts a notch in the door jamb every day.

Bob sacked one of the boys today who has been with us since the first day we came to Sierra Leone. It made me sad even though his offense was a serious one, smoking hashish. We knew something was wrong with him but suspected that it was palm wine. The DC came today and diagnosed the trouble.

You must learn right now what a DC is. This stands for District Commissioner, the chief administrative officer in the country districts of all British possessions. He is generally a fine, tall, handsome, intelligent, humane gentleman. A few are narrow, stuffy, opinionated booze-hounds but, in general, they are very nice men. In the old days of the Empire it was possible for a DC to control an area larger than the whole of Great Britain. Before Pomp and Circumstance went out of style, the DC and his entourage made an impressive sight. He was often accompanied by fifty porters carrying headloads of the finest goods that Fortnum and Mason could produce. When the DC comes now he is always accompanied by a court messenger who acts as his orderly. The messenger immediately puts up the Union Jack so the people will know the Queen's representative is in residence. Today even with his diminished retinue, the DC does not lack dignity. He always manages to produce a rumpled tie to wear at dinner. The Africans are being trained to take over his job and Sierra Leone has several native DCs now.

Santigi, our sanitary engineer (he empties the toilet cans), just called me to come and "lookum Madam!" I went to the window and there were three huge chimpanzees staring in at me. A colony of them live on the mountain behind camp. The camp is surrounded by mango trees as big as oaks and the chimps have come down to see how the crop is progressing. They love mangoes and we can expect an invasion when they are ripe. The chimps don't seem afraid of us at all, possibly because we hide when we see them coming. The big ones weigh more than two hundred pounds.

We have a new steward boy who unfortunately speaks perfect English. Yesterday I told him to investigate an unpleasant smell in the dining room. He came out an hour later while I was sipping a cup of tea with the DC's wife, a proper English woman, and said in perfectly enunciated English, "Madam, the mongoose has shit under the table." The Africans learned much of their English from the British Army and it is not safe to engage them in small talk in mixed company. One evening when we had guests I casually asked one of the boys how his wife was and he launched into a detailed description of the malfunctions of her urino-genital system that made my hair stand on end. Conversation with bushmen is so stimulating that one longs for the haven of clichés.

Love, Mama

Dear Lolly and Suzy,

We were awakened this morning by the night watchman yelling "Teef! Teef!" outside our bedroom window. Bob hastily grabbed his pants and ran up the hill but he was too late. The thief had stolen two large gasoline drums, letting the gas run down the hillside. It costs sixty cents a gallon plus a tedious hundred-eighty-mile haul to get it here. The teef wanted only the drums to store his palm oil in.

Nurse Bard came by today for her weekly clinic. She brought one of her protegées along, a pretty African girl carrying a fat baby. This is her third child and she came along today to invite us to her wedding. Talk about long engagements. She is marrying one of our workers and they will have a Christian wedding under Nurse Bard's supervision.

We drove to the mission hospital yesterday for Bob's typhoid shot which was overdue. Our driver wanted a penicillin shot for his venereal disease, but the doctor refused to give him one until he brought his three wives along for treatment. He muttered all the way home about the high cost of living. Lappia is our best driver because he can drive a Land Rover at maximum speed over potholes three feet deep. He has never been known to give way to another driver, friend or enemy. Bob won't let me drive in Sierra Leone because he says I lack the verve and daring to compete with the local chauffeurs. The game of chicken was invented here. They never swerve out to pass until they can see the pupil of the eye of the oncoming driver.

Did I write that we have another monkey? He is just like a little boy, greedy, destructive, filthy, inquisitive and jealous and we can't help loving him. The trees are full of his relatives and we keep hoping that he will go and join them but he has grown too fond of the beer and peanuts that the Australians feed him.

I think Madam Jenny has gone home now, so I will sneak up to the ironing room and press a few things. I hate for her to know that I don't trust her ironing. She often sets the hot iron down on whatever she is ironing and takes a catnap on the adjoining table, her head pillowed on a stack of clean clothes. I never put anything of mine for which I have a deep feeling in the communal wash. The first week I was here I saw Jenny beating a pale-pink dacron dress over a granite boulder. She uses lots of detergent and rinses lightly so that in the rainy weather when Bob walks along with wet socks, foam rolls out over the tops of his shoes. Miracle fabrics, detergents, hot irons and their various relationships are not clear to Jenny.

Love, Mama

GBANGBAMA
APRIL

Dear Lolly and Suzy,

We now have another woman at camp, Joan Rose, the English wife of our Canadian engineer. Rob follows her around like a faithful dog because she is always cooking goodies for him. She has a fifteen-year-old son at school in England.

106

I hear a delegation coming up the hill from the village, probably the chief asking a small favor. He often sends his messenger up to ask for transport here and there, to palaver with neighboring chiefs, to attend district court or to attend someone's funeral. Wherever he travels his entourage numbers at least fifteen people—his favorite wives and children, his clerk, his speaker and other members of the palace set. We have to use the Dodge power wagon to get them all in.

His last request was to ask Bob to build him a landing strip. This burst of progressive thinking was brought on by his hearing about the new air service in Sierra Leone. If they should come this way he wants to be ready. This new air service consists of one plane which flies from Freetown to Bo to Magbuaka twice a week. It is an early vintage de Haviland Rapide and the wings are partly made of wood. Cynics have been making gloomy predictions about what the white ants are going to do to it after a few weeks in the tropics. This plane has a bathroom scale in the aisle to weigh the passengers and luggage. When you are weighed the pilot points out the seat where your weight can be placed most advantageously. Regular customers don't have to be weighed every flight as their weight is courteously remembered.

If the chief wants a landing strip, we will probably build him one. He looks like a worthless old soak but the DC says he keeps order in his chiefdom, doesn't allow ritual murder and collects the taxes, a very fine record indeed. Nurse Bard says this chiefdom, in spite of its past evil record, is now virtually the Switzerland of the country. The people seek haven here when there are rumors of impending secret-society activity.

But the chief does like his gin. Bob gave him a beautiful wall clock for Christmas and he received it as happily as he would have a fur-lined syrup pitcher. He likes all his presents to be in bottles.

Maybe you two can come out to see us this summer, but if you can't you must go to summer school. No more grass-hoppering around like you have done all your past summers. For the rest of your lives you must be in school or at work. Your father and I are eager to get you out of school and on someone else's payroll.

Love, Mama

Dear Lolly and Suzy,

Tell Mother I was so happy to have a letter by her own hand. In spite of her eighty-odd years she still writes the best and most legible letter in the family. She says her cataracts are getting so bad she can't tell a cow from a cousin and if she lifts her pen while writing she loses her place on the page. Tell her I got her an African walking stick today. It is made of coffee wood with horrible faces carved up and down it—a fine stick for intimidating grandchildren.

Today the Roses and I went to Bo via Mattru and the Land Rover and dugout canoe. It took us four hours to go the fifty miles because we had to chop a couple of trees out of the road which had blown over during the night.

Joan and I were delighted with the town after so many weeks in the bush. Sierra Leone has both a train and an airplane and when we were in Bo we saw both the *station* and the *airport*. The stores close at noon on Saturdays and by the time we got there, we had only forty minutes left to shop. But that is long enough to buy everything we could find that we wanted. Bill made a telephone call to Freetown which was the purpose of our trip. He had to shout so loud to be heard that Joan and I could hear him across the street. The telephone system in this

108

country is enough to convince me that the government should never control anything that must work quickly and efficiently. The Sierra Leone telephone is closed on Sundays and holidays and during the week one can make calls only from eight till twelve and from two till six. But it doesn't matter to me as I have never been able to hear anything on the phone anyway. When you pick up the phone in the Freetown house you can hear the British Broadcasting Company broadcasting its program to West Africa. I don't mean you can hear it vaguely in the background, it is as clear as when you turn on a perfect radio. The perfect connection with the BBC has no ill effect on the mechanics of the phone and it is possible to dial your party with no trouble. But the BBC continues loud and clear and only if you are quick, can you convey your message while the announcer pauses for breath or the musician turns a page. Occasionally the telephone line will be completely dead and you can't even get the BBC. Then the houseboy goes outside and pokes the telephone line with a broom and restores the service. Once more the bushman has proved he is smarter than Americans. Who would ever attempt to fix a phone with a broom in the good old U.S.A.? You will think these are all lies but it is too true. Bob says there's poor phone service because the insulation wears off the wires so quickly in this country and also because with the tremendous rainfall, everything is saturated all the time.

There was a tremendous hatching of flying ants last night. John, Tom and Rob spent a happy evening helping the night watchman catch a jarful. Then he crisped them on the wood stove for a minute and gobbled them up. John and Tom have been nibbling them for some time and Bob and I finally tasted the termites. They have a good, nutlike flavor, and are quite appetizing if you sprinkle them with salt and don't look at them close enough to see their little legs. Nurse Bard encourages the Africans to eat them as they are pure protein, which is sorely lacking in the local diet. There is another delicacy which I can't bring myself to try, large white grubs which live in oil palm trees. These are reputed to make delicious stew with vegetables. Yesterday I saw Bob's clerk taking a hatful home to his wife.

Love, Mama

GBANGBAMA<br>EASTER DAY

Dear Lolly and Suzy,

This morning the Roses and Spencers went down to the village church to celebrate Easter. The pastor gave a very good sermon, first in English for the guests and then "in the vernacular," as he said. Little cards with Dog, Cat, and House printed in Mende were hanging around the walls of the church for, during the week, this building is the schoolhouse. It is a little open shed with thatched roof, earthen floors and rough-hewn benches which fit the anatomy of schoolchildren better than adult churchgoers. The building was crowded with people of all ages in a variety of colorful costumes. A handsome Carmen-like creature swept in after the sermon had begun and seated herself at the feet of the preacher. I noticed that all the latecomers went right to the center of things rather than slinking into the back row as we do. A rough table was used for a pulpit and I wanted to weep when I saw the decorations, a Klim powdered-milk tin filled with flowers, set on a piece of ragged lace. I thought of the thousands of vases in the thousands of attics in America. The floor all around the preacher was crowded with children, and mothers suckled their babies. All the children were quiet and well behaved, including John, Tom and Rob. The surroundings may have been unusual but the message was universal and as well received by Mende as by European. "O, Death, where is thy sting? O, Grave, where is thy victory?"

The ants in Gbangbama carry Easter eggs off as soon as one can hide them, so we did not have an egg hunt. The children were delighted with the three slightly smashed chocolate eggs which I found in Freetown several weeks ago.

We planned to go to Shenge for Easter but we never got there. Shenge is one of the picturesque coastal villages which were thriving slaving and trading posts in the nineteenth century. People only go there now to fish and swim. There are no accommodations except a rough rest house, so we spent three days packing a Land Rover with food, beds, mosquito nets, water, pots, pans and a stove. The houseboy and the cook packed all their gear, too. We started off on Friday and got about thirty miles when we overtook one of the vehicles from camp on the way to Freetown. It had broken down and we had to take the driver back to camp for help. By that time it was too late to go on to Shenge as one must arrive at a campsite by daylight. One needs at least an hour of daylight to organize the defense against ants, snakes and mosquitoes.

Bob decided that since we were a day late, we could not go at all because he had another engagement at the other end of the country in three days. We were mad enough to spit. The children and I unpacked and grumbled, and grumbled and unpacked all day yesterday.

Now I hear that the bridge at Kabati has fallen in and we can't get to Mattru to get the mail. Calm, calm—I mustn't harden my arteries.

Love, Mama

Dear Lolly and Suzy,

We have been having wild storms with wind and lightning. You know I have always found storms exhilarating and have taught my children not to be afraid. But that was before I lived in a little aluminum house that rippled in the wind. I have gone through tornadoes in Alabama and hurricanes in Florida but I was always in a substantial building. Now in my terror, I rush around in the night shouting and shaking everyone to wake them to their peril and they only grunt and roll over and go back to sleep with the rain in their faces. It blows so hard that it comes in under every window. When I lift Rob out of bed, instead of clinging to my skirts in terror and comforting me, he leans against the dresser and sleeps standing up. I have given up seeking company for my nightly vigil and just sit and wring my hands alone while the thunder cracks, the wind roars and the banana trees lie flat on the ground. Our little houses are perched right on the side of the mountain so there is no protection from the wind. They are imbedded in concrete or they would have blown away long ago. These storms always last for several weeks at the beginning and at the end of the rainy season.

I have been reading some British-published "Brer Rabbit" stories to Rob, and the writer says, "Brer Rabbit was sitting rocking on his terrace when Brer Fox came by." Brer Rabbit would never recognize his porch as a terrace. All of the books the children read are English. Beatrix Potter's *Peter Rabbit*, *Thomasina Tittlemouse*, and *Little Pig Robinson*, with their original illustrations, are much better than the American versions. Another book I have just discovered is *Wind in the Willows*. It is delightful. You and Suzy must read it if you haven't. I thought I had read all children's books but when I discovered it, I felt like Keats on first looking into Chapman's Homer.

It is wonderful to have enough time to read and read and read. I am wearing out my eyes and must get glasses when I come home. Bob and I take turns using his.

I have read all of Faulkner since I have been here. I always felt that no one could understand him except me. (Who but an Alabamian would appreciate his description of the scallops eaten out of a wooden fence by a mule, hungry for salt?) Yet camp is full of his books in English paperback editions, left by all the foreigners who have been here. So a true artist must write for all of mankind. Faulkner is a marvelous comedian and at the same time can write so movingly that you feel your heart will break. I wept unashamedly when poor Mink Snopes was cheated on his Coca-Cola and can of sardines by that miserable storekeeper. As for Faulkner's sordid writing, I just ignore that. Your father says I have led such a sheltered life that I will not face the fact that mankind is as wicked as it is.

Rob is about to blast us out of the house with the record player. There is quite a collection of records left here by former tenants. They are not particularly suitable for small fry but Rob likes them, especially "What Do You Do with a Drunken Sailor?" and "Sobbin' Women."

We just heard the biweekly plane fly over from New York to Monrovia. We ran out to watch it go by and imagined it was full of Americans looking down at the wild savages below. As a matter of fact, the only pagan ritual we were observing was drinking a coke and playing a new album from "My Fair Lady."

Bob says you may start getting your passports, visas, yellow-fever shots and smallpox vaccination and *maybe* you can come to see us in June. Surely he will let you come after you have been riddled with shots.

Love, Mama

Dear Lolly and Suzy,

We finally got over to Shenge for a few days. It is a sleepy place with white beaches, coconut palms, and frangipani and bougainvillaea growing rampant over the deserted mission buildings. There is still a pretty, old stone church in use. Most of the natives speak fluent English, a legacy of the departed missionaries. I don't know why the missionaries would ever leave Shenge, but such is their calling. They go ever inland to the worst, most inaccessible places. The nastiest remark that one mission sect can make about another is, "Their missions are all on the railway line."

There is a small island off Shenge with an old fort which is crumbling into the water. John and Tom unearthed a rusty, half-buried cannon decorated with the emblem of George III. We hope to go back there soon and look for pieces of eight.

We have been looking for *Sputnik* or *Explorer* flying across Africa but have had no luck yet. The fathers at the Catholic Mission in Bonthe have seen them once. The mountaintop here is an excellent place to stargaze, undisturbed by reflections from neon lights and airport beacons. This time of year we sit out each night in deck chairs and look into the Southern Cross. On the right are Sirius and Orion and on the left is Virgo. When we get enough energy we are going to turn our chairs around and see what is in the north. The boys make a good thing of their father teaching them astronomy. They want to stay up every night until midnight and think we don't notice that they are usually catching lightning bugs or chasing toads instead of observing the heavens.

A Superintendent of the Colonial Police is spending the weekend with us. (That word "Colonial" has gone out of style so I know this isn't the right title.) He is a young Englishman with a wife, two children, two houseboys, two policemen, a big Black Maria and a Police Launch. This is only an informal visit. I have never met any English people who knew how to travel light. It is a revelation to see a DC go on trek. He has enough beds, pillows, dishes, chairs, pots and pans to stock a hotel. I don't think Americans are nearly as comfort loving as Europeans.

We go on having terrible storms but nobody worries about them but me. An Englishman told me that Milton mentions Sierra Leone storms in *Paradise Lost*. I don't know how he heard about them when nobody ever warned me. The rains have started now so the storms will gradually stop.

Love, Mama

GBANGBAMA
MAY DAY

Dear Lolly and Suzy,

We have lots of overnight guests at Gbangbama because we are at the end of the road and the nearest motel is three thousand miles away. Often we have warning that visitors are coming but that isn't always helpful. An English name can mean an illiterate chief or a Cambridge-educated Creole and an African name can mean a Mende bushman or an Oxford-educated lawyer. If one has rice and bonga laid on to eat, the guest will prefer filet mignon; if one has a fine pork roast, the visitor will be a devout Moslem, so the catering has to be done on the spur of the moment.

Our worst problem is visitors with pets. All Europeans bring at least one and one intrepid lady brought a dog, a cat, a civet cat and a chimp. I have always had so many troublesome, noisy Spencers that I dared not take an animal visiting. I have found that no matter how appealing children and animals are to their owners, other people can take them or leave them, preferring to leave them.

Camp is already filled with animals, and our animals either hate the visitors' animals, snarling and fighting with them all weekend or, worse, they love them, and spend the weekend courting under the dining-room table.

Rob just came in with a rat climbing on his shoulder. I was horrified but he told me that Kamara had put a "medicine" on him and the rat wouldn't bite. Rob carefully rubbed his magic arm against John and Tom so they would be protected too. Whatever the houseboy did works because the rat is as docile as a lamb and I know that he was just caught in the warehouse.

This boy who put the medicine on Rob is high up in the Poro Society, a sort of thirty-third-degree Mason. He has been little corrupted by civilization and knows all the wood, animal and plant lore of the Mende tribe. He is a member of the Snake Society, thus knowing all the kinds of snakes and the remedies for their poisons. When there are plants and flowers that I want from the bush, he always knows where to find them. I showed him the bulb of a gloriosa lily which grows wild in Sierra Leone and asked him to get me some for the yard. He became very agitated and said "No! No! Madam." Evidently only witches display any interest in gloriosa bulbs because they contain a dreadful poison.

I suppose you two will go with your grandma to Jennings Chapel on the fourth Sunday in May to the memorial service.

"All day singing, dinner on the ground, whiskey in the woods and the devil all around!" That is what the devilish boys used to chant when I was a girl. You must not miss that occasion as you have two sets of grandparents buried there as well as hundreds of cousins and Aunt Anne and Uncle Rat. Uncle Rat is the ghost who walks through Grandma's attic now. I never missed a fourth Sunday in May at Jennings Chapel until I was married. I will think of you all stuffing fried chicken, chocolate cake and pecan pie while I am eating corn beef and tough grey peas from a can.

Are you assembling your wardrobe for your African trip? Your clothes must be cool, packable and washable. It is all right to wear shorts in Freetown but I wouldn't in the bush. The ladies may be completely bare from the waist up, but they are very modest about showing their legs. Concentrate on looking *pretty* rather than *smart*. Looking smart is for the birds and those grotesque hags in *Vogue*. Your dresses must be pretty colors and pleasing to the touch as the African ladies will want to feel them. Wear comfortable shoes—no pecking around in sharp-toed spikes, especially when you are sightseeing in London.

Suzy, we never got the insurance paper you sent. About half of our mail goes astray. Of last year's subscription to *Life* magazine, I got two copies. Now I subscribe only to highbrow things with no pictures and they are less likely to end up in the hut of some indigene. Tell everyone never to mail us any packages as they will either be stolen or charged a prohibitive customs rate.

Please bring a few packages of seeds to infuse new life into the flowers and vegetables here. The zinnias, eggplants and tomatoes are so small.

Love, Mama

Dear Lolly and Suzy,

Your father will attend to your tickets from here and mail them to you. The tentative route is New York, London, Lisbon, Las Palmas and Freetown. Las Palmas is in the Canary Islands off North Africa—this was Columbus' jumping off place for the New World.

You will leave Birmingham about July 2 and stay in New York that night, then leave for London the next day. Call the London office if you need anything. Your hotel reservations have been made and all of Great Britain has been alerted that you are coming. Our friends, the Mckinneys, will meet you and show you around London.

Travel light. Remember that sometime and somewhere you will have to carry, unaided, every bag you have. Porters are absent when you need them, and hundreds will clamor to help you when you have only a camera and makeup bag to carry.

Don't bring a sample of everything from the U.S.A. The basic needs of mankind are the same the world over and you will be able to satisfy yours in Europe and Africa. The only things you really need are money, passports, health cards and a demijohn of drinking water—if you could figure out a way to carry it. Everything else you can find, even Kleenex.

Bring a camera so you can take pictures of each other feeding pigeons in Trafalgar Square. Be wary of those birds as they defaced my hat and knocked it completely off my head. Take plenty of warm clothes for London. That North Sea wind has no respect for July and is as eager to freeze you then as in January.

Here is the list of things we would like for you to bring us: some Mickey Mouse comics, some bubble gum, some striped toothpaste, a fish gaff and two medium salt-water trolling spoons. A sporting-goods store will have the latter. Bob says bring only the sharp end of the gaff as we can supply the dull end here. Oh boy, can we ever.

You must get your antimalarial pills and start taking them at once. Have your bloodstream armed and ready to fight the moment you set foot in the White Man's Grave. I can't wait for you to see Africa—this limbo between the stone and atomic ages. Lolly, I am so glad you are studying anthropology, botany, biology and zoology—this is where it all began, "the very navel of the earth."

We have another pet, a small genet cat who looks like a leopard. His fur is soft and beautiful and Bob wants to find another one and start a fur farm. The genet cat is a night animal, sleeping in the house all day and coming out to play when we are in bed. He runs in and out of the mosquito net, looking so cunning and sweet, then suddenly he will clamp his razor-sharp teeth on your finger. He purrs like an ordinary kitten but our little house cat refuses to be fooled by this wolf in leopard's clothing and has nothing to do with him. The genet cat is only half as big as a house cat and eats nothing but raw meat, fingers preferred.

The Police Superintendent just sent John and Tom a present, a wondrous pocket knife with all these things folded within: two knife blades, a spoon, a fork, scissors, a bottle opener, a screw driver, a leather punch, a can opener and a saw blade. The boys have cut, pierced, scratched and sawed every finger and knuckle of both hands but they are still hard at it, determined to try out every tool.

Love, Mama

Dear Lolly and Suzy,

I just got your cable saying "No Money." Darn this postal system. We have sent you two checks that have not arrived. Thieves won't be able to cash them but it is such an infernal nuisance to be forever losing mail. Bob cabled you to borrow from Grandma. We don't have time to cable money as that would involve a trip to Freetown. We could send a telegram but sometimes that takes three or four days and we have found that it is quicker to drive down to Freetown. Thinking about local communications will make me tense if I am not careful. Just now I am frothing at the mouth and biting scallops out of the window louvers. It was a sad day when they gave up the cleft stick and the talking drums for communication.

Remember to wear flat, friendly shoes. Pretend to be more naïve and ignorant than you are; ask lots of questions and you will have no trouble anywhere. There is nothing the human race enjoys so much as giving advice to ignorant people.

Remember that Londoners always drive on the wrong side of the street and never step off a curb without looking in both directions. Use the little map I drew for you with all the sightseeing trails running out from your hotel. Always take a bath early in the evening as the hot water often gives out in European hotels. Once in Rome after eight o'clock the chambermaid took the handles off my hot-water taps and hid them until morning.

When you arrive in Sierra Leone, Bob will meet you at the airport and the boys and I will wait at the Freetown wharf. I can't greet you looking my best after that long ride across the bay with your brothers. Besides the trip costs a pound for each of us.

We are counting the minutes until you arrive. No matter how repulsive or obnoxious guests are at Gbangbama, we are delighted to see them, so you can't imagine how elated we are at the thought of your coming. You can have your own private little aluminum house next door to ours and you won't have to wash a dish or make a bed or sweep a floor. You will love it for a while, then—well, you have so much to learn.

Love, Mama

# Two Months Later

Dear Lolly and Suzy,

The two months you were here seemed like two weeks. When we arrived back at camp after seeing you off, the sight of your little empty house started me snuffling. John said, "Don't cry, Mama. Sew on labels," and that is what I am doing.

He and Tom get more enthusiastic every day about boarding school and I am putting name tapes in all their clothes. We are lucky that the mission school has room for them and will take them.

The boys are delighted with the opulence of their wardrobes. They have never seen so much new underwear, and each of them has three pairs of shoes at the same time—and dressing gowns, yet!

Lolly, did you get home with your jar of lungfish? I hope we preserved them properly and your biology professor appreciated our efforts. Your house still reeks of bromoform. I must slip Nurse Bard's hypodermic needle back to the dispensary before she finds out that we have been injecting mudskippers with it.

We are having severe thunderstorms again and Bob now shares my distress as he was knocked down by a bolt of lightning yesterday. He stepped out of the shower, drying himself and all of a sudden he was lying on the floor, naked as a jaybird, kicking his feet feebly. I was at the window watching the storm and when I turned around and saw him making a spectacle of himself, I shouted, "Stop acting like a fool when I am so frightened!" I didn't realize the poor man had been struck. The bolt hit the house, but I was dry and had shoes on, so it didn't hurt me. It had no ill effect on Bob other than to make him resolve to stop bathing until the dry season comes, two months hence. During the storm, balls of fire were dancing all over the mountaintop and through the Mess where the children were playing. I will never use that expression, "Balls of Fire," lightly again.

Rob misses you terribly. You were such pushovers for his every demand. He is now sitting in the middle of his bed polishing his shoes.

Love, Mama

GBANGBAMA<br>SEPTEMBER

Dear Lolly and Suzy,

We took John and Tom to school on Tuesday. It is at Kabala, about two hundred miles away in the northern part of the country near the Guinea border. They were delighted with the school and the twenty-two pupils, all children of missionaries except John and Tom and one African child. The staff consists of the houseparents, the school nurse and two teachers from Indiana. I liked them all, and was happy to entrust my little savages to them.

The country in the north is high and open and the roads aren't green tunnels like they are near Gbangbama. There are great granite hills and the school sits on top of one of them. You can look across the country to Sierra Leone's highest peak, almost seven thousand feet high.

The parents had all gathered from their far-off stations to

bring the children to school, some walking as many as thirty miles to get to a road. We enjoyed their lively conversation about everyday living. They are energetic pioneer types who can turn their hand to every sort of work. Some were middle-aged people who had been born in Sierra Leone of missionary parents. They were all keen hunters and Bob listened with his mouth open while one man told of how many elephants he had killed, one with tusks over seven feet long. He hunts the elephants only when they are damaging the African crops. The missionary's description of the natives dismembering an elephant was the funniest story I have heard. When the beast is dead they swarm upon him in a burst of joy, everyone's machete swinging wildly to cut off or out a choice bit of meat. For several days they crawl in and out of the carcass, hacking and chopping until every scrap of elephant has disappeared. The native laws very sensibly allow no law suits to be brought for wounds received at an elephant kill. Luckily, the missionary's wife is a nurse so she can patch everyone up.

On the trip to Kabala I added two more things to my list of peculiar African specimens—a tortoise who hurries and a whydah bird. We saw this tortoise zooming across the road and I couldn't believe my eyes. The whydah bird is only a few inches long and has plumes sweeping out from the back a foot long. I never saw this bird except in flight so I can't imagine how he manages this huge plume when he lands. Someone told me the bird grows the plume only when courting.

This part of the country is predominantly Moslem. On the verandahs of many of the houses we saw small boards with Arabic characters written on them. These are koranic schools where little boys and girls learn verses from the Koran. They are not taught to read and write, but lately, under the growing influence of Cairo, Islamic missionaries are coming into Sierra Leone and opening proper schools.

The Fula tribe grows many cattle here as there are grasslands for grazing and fewer tsetse flies than in Mende country. The Fulas have milk, butter and cheese, unheard-of delicacies among the Mende people. Driving on the dusty road to Kabala we saw bags of curd tied to the bumpers of mammy wagons. By the time the mammy wagon reaches Freetown, all the whey is shaken out and there is a fine bag of cottage cheese—encrusted with dust.

You know the weakness I have for gathering up dried cow piles to put in geranium pots. The instant I saw cows I started looking for cow piles but not one was to be seen. A missionary explained that cow dung was highly valued as a weatherproofing material for walls and floors and was never used for fertilizer. Just as the Mendes do, the Fulas entreat their soil to be fertile with charms and verses from the Koran rather than with nitrogen.

It is so quiet at Gbangbama without John and Tom. Bob says children are just like women—it is hell to live with them but worse to live without them.

I want you to send me a Christmas box this year and it should be mailed in October. Send cornbread mix, cranberry sauce, pecans and cake mixes. We will have a turkey from England but I must make cornbread stuffing to prove my loyalty to all the Alabama cooks that begat me.

Love, Mama

GBANGBAMA
OCTOBER

Dear Lolly and Suzy,

The doctor from Mattru told us a gruesome tale today. He spent the weekend with the DC in Pujehun and while he was there a messenger came with the news that a child had been killed by a baboon in an isolated village. The doctor went along with the DC to investigate and found the victim, a nine-year-old girl, had been murdered and slashed with a machete to simulate baboon scratches. Her spleen and the layer of fat on her abdomen were missing. These are choice ingredients for making a powerful medicine.

An investigation has been started but it will probably peter out from lack of witnesses. The villagers were numb with terror. If they do get any people to come forward, the DC will have a medicine of his own mixed which the witnesses take when they are sworn. It is a harmless mixture made of ashes, pepper, water, rice, etc. The witness takes a spoonful and swears the following oath: "I (name of witness) swear by this medicine to speak the truth, the whole truth and nothing but the truth. Should I tell a lie, if I go to the farm, may a snake bite me. If I travel by canoe, may the canoe sink, and my belly be swollen. I swear by my liver, my lungs, my kidneys and my heart that should I tell a lie, may I die suddenly." These swears are administered in the Mende language, of course, and are used in the present-day courts when the witness is illiterate, which is most of the time. The people abide by the oath unless they can afford, secretly, to have a witch doctor with a more powerful medicine than the DC's to "pull the swear." This means to nullify the first oath. If they can afford the witch doctor's medicine, they can lie to the DC with impunity.

These occurrences are our chief topic of conversation around camp, but both the missionaries and the government officials are reluctant to discuss ritual murder. I suppose it makes them feel that their sweat and tears are shed in vain. But when you think that ritual murders were common fifty years ago around such thriving modern cities as Accra, the progress of Africa seems phenomenal. Just think how long it took us to graduate from our Druid human sacrifice to our present atomic sacrifice.

Now that I have the boys in school, I have lost my main excuse for coming home, so I may be here for years. I was so depressed today that I planted a coconut tree which takes nine years to come to fruition. I won't be depressed tomorrow because it is mail day and I will get letters from you and John and Tom. The boys will write regularly as they are forced to every Sunday afternoon.

Love, Mama

Dear Lolly and Suzy,

Suzy, don't worry about your terrible grades the first six weeks. Every university concentrates on making the freshman realize his stupidity. That is the beginning of your education.

Lolly, your letter about parasites was enchanting. Each time we get one of your erudite epistles, we feel a new symptom and rush to our copy of *Manson's Tropical Diseases* to see if we can find it illustrated. We call this our Jolly Jungle Book and place it on the bedside table of all unwanted guests. It is liberally illustrated with victims of Aleppo boils, Madura foot, gangosa and beri-beri. However (I tell myself), it is rare for Europeans to get these diseases. Of all the missionaries I know who have been here for years, living under the most primitive conditions, in close proximity to the natives, none has had anything worse than malaria.

We have had one case of sleeping sickness at camp this year, an African laborer who recovered after two months' treatment. A few weeks ago one of the laborers came to work with sores all over him, and Bob, thinking he may have had smallpox, sent him home and told him to go to the doctor in Mattru. The next day he was back in camp and Bob was furious and drove him off the hill. After he had gone the watchman told Bob that the man had been hiding in the woods all night because the people had driven him out of the village. Your father, filled with remorse, sent a Land Rover to find him and take him to Mattru. The doctor diagnosed his ailment as smallpox, built an isolation hut for him near the hospital, got an immune African to nurse him and then the wretched patient ran away. Now he is back in Gbangbama exposing everyone to smallpox. A government man is here today vaccinating anyone he can catch.

When we went to Kabala we saw the UNICEF doctor who is head of the leprosy team in Sierra Leone. He goes around the country, diagnoses the cases and leaves the treatment in the hands of the various mission hospitals. One of the nurses told me that there were over a hundred cases in her area but only forty of them come regularly for treatment. The medicine is free but to be treated successfully the patient must come once a week for two years.

I must stop writing about these depressing things and turn on the radio and hear something really depressing. Africa is bombarded with propaganda day and night from Radio Moscow, Radio Peking and Radio Prague. Their announcers speak English with an American accent and I always think it is the Voice of America until the news becomes too warped. I am afraid the Africans go on thinking it is the Voice of America.

Love, Mama

Dear Lolly and Suzy,

I am so angry with my houseboy I could bash his head in. His child died last night and he never told me that the child was sick. He has been sick for a week and there was plenty of time to take him to the doctor. The child was five, old enough to have a chance for survival in this miserable place.

My houseboy depends on the local medicine man even though he is a Christian who has been to school and is literate. He is the very fool who told me that there is a big snake who goes around Gbangbama every night, clucking like a hen, calling the souls of children. If the soul goes outside, the snake eats it and the child dies.

The fatalistic African thinks that he has little control over his sickness or health—evil spirits will either get you or they won't get you. Rather than taking care of his body, he devotes his time and money to propitiating evil spirits. We always ask *why* when someone dies, but the African never does. When you enquire the reason for someone's death, the stock answer is, "He fall down," meaning he just stopped living. The Mendes believe in several souls that wander around and death seems less fearful to them than to civilized man. From talking to the servants, I gather that the witch doctor spends most of his time trying to keep these capricious souls in their proper abodes. If one is not buried properly his soul does not go to the other world but flits around getting into living people, causing chills and fever, broken legs and blindness. A live man's soul also wanders around when he is asleep, so you must never wake a man suddenly, else his soul may not have time to get back into his body. One also has a soul in his shadow. Your shadow must be guarded very carefully in the middle of the day when it is weak—stay away from enemies and strange villages around midday. The shadow soul renews its strength during the night when it lies down in the shadow of the great god, night. Notice how big and strong the shadow is in the early morning.

I must stop thinking of such things and go dig in my garden. I am so glad you both like gardening. It will be a comfort to you in your old age. One can have such an exotic garden in Africa. I have coffee, cocoa, bananas, cashew, avocado, papaya, mango, guava, orange, grapefruit, lime, breadfruit and almond trees. There are four kinds of bananas: yellow ones, red ones, small two-inch ones and long twelve-inch ones. The latter are plantains which we fry as a substitute for sweet potatoes. I also grow ginger, peanuts, sesame seeds, pineapples and five kinds of hot peppers.

The garden boy is a local farmer who is supposed to know what he is doing, but seldom does his ability coincide with my wishes. I never know where his helpfulness is going to strike next. He cut down all my mint bed and planted half an acre of hot peppers. When I complained, he cut down all the peppers and planted half an acre of mint. I wish I had some connections with a chewing-gum factory, I would like to supply their mint.

The natives are so fond of hot peppers that I have to be ever vigilant or the garden would turn into a vast pepper plantation. The garden boy loves to transplant things, whisking up radishes, lettuce and beans, moving them from place to place before they can get their osmosis going from the previous move. Thank heaven for things that grow on trees or we would starve.

Love, Mama

Dear Lolly and Suzy,

Sierra Leone is a paradise for scientific study. You must tell all your young friends who seek immortality in science that this is one of the places to find it. It is still possible to discover a bird, a plant, a disease or an insect that has not been classified. My being here is such a waste. I don't have patience or sense enough to collect even these beautiful butterflies that fly in and out of my coffee.

Rob has had another bout with malaria. He got overtired during our last trip to Freetown and the smallest thing will trigger an attack. The mission doctor told me that a cold, an infected scratch or even a fall off a bicycle could bring it on among the Africans who are in a perpetual state of low resistance.

We drove up to Kabala to see John and Tom this week. I have had an uneasy feeling about them because I was afraid that the only people who could love small boys were their mothers. I was afraid if we sent them away they might be put in irons. We found them as happy as clams without a complaint of any kind. We went panting up to see them, breathless with anticipation, and they hardly had time to speak to us they were so busy with their own affairs. You should see the startling change that six weeks has made in their table manners. They both watched poor Rob like a hawk and corrected him every minute for using the wrong implement, licking his fingers or talking too loud. Tom told him, "We have two voices here, one for inside and one for outside." This, from that raucous Tom! John pulled my chair out and seated me at the table and they both said "Thank you," "Excuse me" and "Please" until Bob and I wondered if we had the wrong children.

Suzy, Tom got your letter and asked for your address so he could answer. You must have bribed him. I assured him that we would send all his letters straight to you if he sent them to us first. We don't want any of his meager news diluted by being sent in two directions. The body of his letters is the statement that he and John are well and that he hopes Daddy, Rob and I are well also. Anything other than this is rare and we consider pure pay dirt. Even though it is a product of forced labor, the mail from Kabala is the highlight of my week. Don't underestimate the value of your epistles, either. I have a hollow feeling in my stomach for hours if I don't get a letter from the U.S.A. in Saturday's mail. Now that it is too late, I think of all the letters I should have written in my life to people in lonely, faraway places.

You remember that I wrote you how callous I thought the Mendes were for not burying their dead babies but just putting them on the refuse heap? Since then I have read a book on Mende customs and I find that their refuse heap is considered a place of honor. It isn't filled with the trivia of our profligate society but is the final resting place of their beloved possessions when they are too old to be serviceable—the possessions that mean life itself to the Mendes—worn-out fishtraps, machetes, baskets. If a dead baby is placed among these the family is assured of the spirits bringing them another baby. Every time I belittle a strange custom, I find a sensible reason for it. I have so much to learn.

Love, Mama

Dear Lolly and Suzy,

I had a horrible dream last night that Lolly had bought a mink coat, probably brought on from my worry that you spend too much money for clothes—not too much compared with other people, but too much for Spencers. Please learn to wear your clothes out before getting more, an unheard-of thing in America.

I often have nightmares about my missing children. I dream of John and Tom drowning, being bitten by cobras or falling off cliffs while you two are buying Thunderbirds, fur coats and stereo equipment.

We took Bill Rose to Freetown for an appendectomy this week. He got sick quickly and we rushed off, leaving our Sunday dinner in the oven. I had a beautiful pumpkin chiffon pie which I could not bear to leave behind and as I got into the car, I turned it upside-down all over us. We drove to Freetown, left the Roses and drove back the same day. Three hundred and sixty miles of steady driving in this country is enough to shake one to jelly.

Bill is getting along nicely but Bob is the only white man at camp now and the VIPs are coming out from London, Melbourne and Pittsburgh next week. Bob is all broken out in a rash, probably from nerves. Our best driver drove our newest Land Rover off a bridge fifty miles from camp in one direction and the Dodge power wagon is broken down seventy miles in the other direction. Unless a European is circulating around camp all the time, the Africans stop their work and go to sleep. How can poor Bob circulate and attend to everything at the same time? We have given Rob a supervisory job of exhorting the Africans to do their best for dear old Pittsburgh Plate Glass. Foolish little Yankee that he is, he loves to work.

If I didn't restrain him, he would be in the hot sun all day carrying drilling samples, cutting bush or mixing concrete.

I have just read an interesting article in the Freetown paper. Quote: "The Minister of Finance stated yesterday that a minister going on leave cannot have the passages of more than a combination of four persons altogether paid for from public funds. Thus he can have passages for one wife and three children or two wives and two children; he clearly cannot claim for four wives." Well, this is one problem Washington doesn't have yet.

All of the ministers are now African and are from Sierra Leone, yet they are given paid leave to go to England just as the former English ministers were. I don't see how the country can afford it. Sierra Leone is about the size of West Virginia. Can you imagine the people there paying for their state officials even to go to Washington, much less paying for a trip abroad? The officials would be tarred and feathered if they dared suggest it.

Love, Mama

Dear Lolly and Suzy,

Happy birthday, Lolly. Twenty seems so old for you. Rob was happy that you remembered it was his birthday, too. His present arrived in time and Joan Rose baked him a birthday cake so he had a fine day.

We have six VIPs visiting us this week, two from England, two from Australia and two from the States. Joan and I have tried to please them all. Some like early dinner; some like late dinner; some like to drink; some are teetotalers; some like tea and some like coffee. English, American or Australian food—which shall it be?

They were all quite agreeable so maybe we pleased them all. They congratulated me on being so cheerful and adaptable while living in the bush. After that, how could I say to them, "Give Africa back to the elephants. I want to go home and see Lolly and Suzy!"

Bob says I would hate a humdrum, comfortable life no matter how much I protest the fate of a miner's wife. When I contemplate suicide, I read in my bankbook. Solvency is a state not to be deprecated.

We have had some interesting visitors from Freetown—the Minister of Mines and his wife who is an American Negro. He is a Sierra Leonean who was educated at McGill University in Montreal. They are charming, intelligent, urbane people, and it is annoying to me that I have been denied by custom knowing any educated Negroes before. I am the poorer for it.

Love, Mama

GBANGBAMA
DECEMBER

Dear Lolly and Suzy,

John and Tom will be home for Christmas vacation in three days. At camp there will be five Spencers, Joan and Bill Rose and Harry Wilson, the English engineer. Rob loves Mr. Wilson because he makes him out a pay slip with an African name and lets him collect three pence on pay day. He calls him Ali Bhama because of his deep-south accent.

We have decided that Rob must learn to swim, so we are going to make him a pool on the mountainside. Our water supply is pure and clean and we will make a small pool

138

below the water catchment, just big enough for him and his dog. We can't swim in the streams here and we don't go to the ocean often enough for him to learn. All the villages are built on streams, the upper part used for drinking, the middle for washing and bathing and the lower part for a toilet. This would be a fine arrangement if there were only a few villages, but there are thousands, so every stream is polluted. When I remarked to Nurse Bard how surprisingly clean the villages were considering their lack of plumbing, she explained their sanitary system to me.

Madam Rose and I have put up a long string in the Mess to hang our Christmas cards on, but we have received only one. Bob bought a synthetic tree in Freetown which Rob decorates every day. We are going to get John and Tom wristwatches for Christmas and Rob will get two laying hens. He is mad about poultry. You remember how he loved gathering eggs in Alabama. We have one old rooster at camp and Rob follows him around making comfortable nests everywhere, but he hasn't laid the first egg. We have been promised two laying hens by Mrs. Baker from the Mattru mission.

Lolly, don't think of matrimony so much. There are many fish in the sea and I want you to fish a long time. Don't get married because it is fashionable. I expect my son-in-law to be a lifetime investment. I want him to be intelligent, industrious, moral, healthy, witty and able to support a wife. This creature can't be found easily.

Love, Mama

Dear Lolly and Suzy,

I am thirty-nine years old today, my last birthday for the next ten years. We baked a birthday cake and Christmas cookies out of the mixes you sent. With John and Tom here we have three little tongues licking out every mixing bowl.

The doctor from Mattru, his wife and three small daughters spent the weekend with us. We went down to the church in Gbangbama on Sunday. The doctor prayed the main prayer, with a man from the village repeating each sentence in Mende. A lady sat in front of me in a gay lappa imprinted with pictures of the Russian satellite and the dog who was the first celestial navigator. I could hardly keep my mind on the sermon for marveling at the wonders of science and commerce —this space dog already immortalized on a West African lappa. Incredible.

I sat looking at all the silver jewelry in the congregation, wondering how much of it was made from our spoons. The camp has bought dozens of sets of silver but the spoons disappear before we can get them on the table.

I am reading an English cookbook for the tropics. There are recipes for cow-heel jelly, sour-sop fool, mango fool, battered eggs, green bacon, pickled hump, ox-cheek mould and soused local fish. (I see a lot of the latter.) I am going to make sour-sop fool as we can get both sweet and sour sops in the village. The fruit is the size of a large pear, green and rough on the outside with a sweet, tart pulp inside. My two favorite dishes from Sierra Leone are palaver sauce and groundnut stew. Palaver sauce, to be served on rice, is made of beef, tripe, fish, palm oil, hot peppers, onions and local greens. Groundnut stew is even better—groundnuts are peanuts. It is made of chicken, hot peppers, eggplant, pumpkin

140

and onions, all cooked together and thickened with crushed, roasted peanuts. This is also served on rice. Sometime I cheat and use peanut butter for the thickening. This saves hours of work—roasting the peanuts and rolling them out on the bread board until they turn to peanut butter. Some English people call peanut butter "monkey-nut paste."

The harmattan is blowing and it is very cold tonight. Maybe it will get down to eighty degrees for Christmas.

Love, Mama


GBANGBAMA
CHRISTMAS

Dear Lolly and Suzy,

Christmas with these thieving, pagan Africans is a revelation. They all claim to be Christians at this time of year and expect to be compensated therefore. On the seventh of December at one thirty in the morning a group of carolers came up to serenade us. We told them that it was much too late in the night and much too early in the month to be singing carols but they paid no attention and burst into song with their faces pressed against our bedroom windows. Africans can sleep all day but we have to get up at six in the morning so we were furious. However one hardly likes to blast off with a shotgun when Christ's birth is being extolled. We didn't give them a dash, which is why they came, and we threatened to sack the night watchman if he ever woke us again at that hour.

I just had a note from the garden boy saying, "Madam, we Christians is too close this time of year. Please borry me a pound." Bob gave the workers a bag of rice and a goat for their Christmas present. We just went out and had a look at the preparations for their feast. There is a twelve-gallon black pot of rice and another of goat and vegetables. The goat was singed instead of skinned, and they put all of him in the pot except his hair. They did clean the entrails first, then put them back in the pot.

John, Tom and Rob got up at 2:00 A.M. to see what Father Christmas brought them. (English children say Father Christmas.) The moon was so bright they must have thought it was daylight. I awoke and found them gone to the Mess where we have the tree. I descended on them like a witch and drove them back to bed where they stayed just long enough for me to go back to sleep.

I picked a pineapple out of my garden which is one compensation for having Christmas in Africa. It weighed almost ten pounds and the cook said, "Na fine English pineapple!" The good varieties of all local fruit have come from the agricultural station run by Englishmen, so everything of good quality is called "English," be it fruit, fowl or fish. A walnut is called an "English groundnut." An enterprising Mende in the bush is growing guinea pigs and selling them for food. He calls them English rats.

Suzy, I am afraid you use your studying time for partying and your sleeping time for studying. You will get bags under your eyes and have coffee nerves if you don't get enough sleep.

Love, Mama

GBANGBAMA<br>DECEMBER

Dear Lolly and Suzy,

We got very little mail at Christmas. Any rush is unthinkable to the Africans, so the post office did the same amount of work as usual. The extra Christmas mail will all be delivered about February. An English girl told me that she has gotten Christmas cards in Sierra Leone as late as June. The post office closed early on the twenty-fourth with stacks of mail and packages unsorted.

One nice thing about Christmas in Gbangbama is that we are not dead broke afterward because there is so little to buy. Another helpful financial aspect of the bush is that we don't have to subscribe to all the autumn drives of the Heart, Lung, Liver, Brain and Kidney Funds in America. After living in this harsh society and seeing that people do survive, I will always be a bit dubious about supporting these drives to save the various internal organs of prosperous Americans.

We had a thrill last night when driving back from Momaligi. Bob, John, Joan and I were in the Land Rover and we saw a leopard in the road who ran straight in front of the car for about fifty yards. Bob gave chase as fast as he could drive and we passed right over the top of him. We didn't feel the slightest bump, so the vehicle must not have touched him at all. We stopped and looked around cautiously but there was nothing. About three miles farther down the road we ran over a large civet cat. Both times Joan was so busy watching the cat that she forgot to hold on and when the brakes were slammed on she was thrown to the floor with a basket of oranges over her head. By the time we got to camp we were all in hysterics and laughing like a drain. Bill Rose thought we must have been drinking. Our leopard tale only confirmed his belief. Finally John convinced him that it was all true. Bob and John—being such keen hunters—were disappointed not to have hit the leopard but I was so glad he got away. It would have been sickening to hit that beautiful, gold creature.

I heard a good story in Bonthe today. "Under communism, man exploits man. Under capitalism, the reverse is true."

Love, Mama

143

Dear Lolly and Suzy,

We had a fine house party last weekend with some invited guests and some who just appeared from stranded Land Rovers and launches. There were three Frenchmen, two Greeks, an Indian (a real Indian, not a red one), a Scotsman and five Englishmen. We played bridge and Scrabble in several languages and one of the Englishmen played folk music on his accordion. The favorite song for all nationalities was "Everybody Likes Saturday Night."

Tom has just quoted a poem for us out of one of his books: "If you hear a panther, Don't anther." Now we are all making rhymes about African animals. "An otter, Likes watter." "Leopard tensed, Bushman minced." "Spiders in furs, Are tarantulurs."

Rob's two hens have been laying every day and he is saving the eggs for hatching. Once a missionary brought a setting of eggs back from America and two of the eggs hatched. Rob's hens are descendants of those two American eggs.

You two should be here now because we have a handsome English bachelor in the office. We hope that he will work, that is, work according to North American standards. The moment Englishmen set foot here, most of them turn into gentlemen of leisure and want to spend their time supervising the "cheap" African labor. Local labor, being so unproductive, is the most expensive in the world. A white man here, to accomplish anything, must work twice as hard as he would at home but most of the Europeans we know come to work a little late, leave work a little early and take two hours off for lunch.

We went to Bonthe yesterday and saw a crocodile sunning himself along the creek. We also saw three otters sitting along the bank eating clams. A woman in Freetown has an otter for a pet and they are adorable, so cunning and devilish. When she takes him visiting to a strange house, he immediately goes in the bathroom and splashes all the water out of the toilet.

Suzy, I am perturbed about paying sixteen hundred dollars a year to have you study folk dancing and freshman orientation. You can learn these subjects for considerably less money at your old mother's knee. I realize that you can't change the curriculum of state universities, but always be on the lookout for courses that will educate you. A few will crop up now and then.

Love, Mama

Dear Lolly and Suzy,

John and Tom have gone back to school and Rob is so forlorn. He has spent the morning following a labor gang around the camp. He told me that two of them have newly shaven heads; one was shaved because of the death of his mother, and the other because he had been put in the block (jail). Rob knows more about the Mendes than any other member of the family. His best friend is Tommy Tao, who is "Congoli" in all the village dances. Congoli is a comic devil who is supposed to be the ugliest man in Sierra Leone. The dancers never divulge their identity, so Tommy won't admit that he is Congoli but he is making Rob a Congoli mask. We will bring it home and hang it on the porch to frighten off salesmen.

We have just returned from Moyamba, haunted by the usual disasters that driving entails in this country. These darned people have been seeing vehicles for years, yet their behavior is still unpredictable when they are overtaken on the

145

road. It was our luck to meet an unusually volatile group of pedestrians today and, in spite of our proceeding cautiously, great havoc was wrought. One small girl with a bucket of water on her head started to sprint down the road the moment she heard us. When she decided we were gaining, she plunged into the bush, catching the bucket on a limb, and pouring the water down her back. A few miles farther we blew the horn gently at a boy rolling a hoop and he dived down a ten-foot embankment, leaving the hoop rolling down the road. Near the next village we came up behind a man on a bicycle who jumped straight in the air and came down on his behind in the road while the bicycle shot off without him. As we drove into Moyamba over the thirty-foot-high bridge, a man who was crossing sprang up on the railing to jump in so we wouldn't hit him. By this time Bob was exhausted and furious with all these crises and he jumped out of the car and yelled at the man to come on across. He sheepishly climbed down from the railing and crossed but I was afraid that Bob was going to kick him into the river.

The DC told us that many of the bushmen are afraid because they believe that white men go around the country in cars and gather up Africans to eat. The standard bugaboo for African children is "The white man will get you!" The DC said that he once stopped on a bridge to take some pictures and a woman who was crossing ran screaming off in terror. She dropped her child off her back when she plunged into the underbrush and the DC went running after her to help. His pursuit confirmed her worst suspicions and she ran twice as fast and screamed twice as loud. The DC's driver finally called him back and convinced him that the lady didn't need any help.

Did I say that American roads were nerve racking?

Love, Mama

Dear Lolly and Suzy,

I know my letter writing has been erratic lately because I am homesick and tired of everything and everybody. Even Rob is getting peculiar. Now he is chasing his hens around the dining-room table. Before people come to West Africa they should be screened as rigidly as a submarine crew. I am just getting end-of-tourish, as one of my friends described her waspishness. I have been here fourteen months this tour and that is too long, but Bob has been so busy he couldn't get away.

Everyone tells stories about people who have been here too long and "gone bush." My favorite is about a little man who thinks he is a poached egg. The thoughtful hostesses around the country always provide him with a piece of toast to sit on.

When I am homesick all the problems of Africa depress me. It makes me sad to see the African abandon his tribal customs and take on the white man's ways without the initiative or understanding to accept his responsibilities. The African wants roads, hospitals, bicycles and penicillin but he doesn't know how we "civilized" people are enslaved to pay for these things. When the Africans get their independence they will have to give up lots of pastimes that are dear to their hearts —swinging in their hammocks all day, dancing all night and suing their neighbors when they are bored.

Last week I heard a seven-year-old boy threaten to "summons" a man for laughing at him when he fell out of his canoe. What seven-year-old in America would know what "summons" meant? Everyone in Sierra Leone is constantly suing or being sued. There are two systems of law in the country, English law and Native law. The native courts operate at village level and are made up of the chief and other prominent citizens. Each man pleads his own case and no lawyers are allowed in Native courts. Magistrates' courts, operating under English law, are held in the larger towns, and try serious crimes or any suit involving a European.

Bob's poor clerk is involved in a case now because he tried to do someone a favor. He was asked by three of the laborers to order watches for them from a mail-order house in London. The laborers gave the clerk one pound each for the three watches, but the store, being out of one-pound watches, substituted two better watches. Now three people want two watches and they won't accept the clerk's explanation and accuse him of "teefing" the third watch.

John and Tom continue to write that they are very happy in Kabala. There is a vast contrast between Rob's mining camp and their mission-school upbringing. With all the "Old Coasters" that pass through Gbangbama Rob has learned to be an enthusiastic practitioner of loose living. He plays liar dice, watches the papers for the football pools and puts a tot of gin in his lemonade if we don't watch him. John and Tom are not exposed to worldliness in any form. Maybe you two middle-of-the-roaders can weld us into a homogeneous unit to present to Grandma when we come home. John and Tom accept their rigid discipline so happily that it proves to me discipline is what children want. Starting right now I am going to be a good disciplinarian. You two are going to send me a balanced financial statement every month and Rob is going to stop feeding butter to the mongoose.

It really keeps me stepping to answer the boys' questions about different religious sects. Sierra Leone has Catholics, Moslems, leftish Protestants, rightish Protestants and middle-of-the-road Protestants, and they all have peculiar customs as you will find when you try to explain them to small boys. They want to know why I wear lipstick when Willie's mother thinks it a deplorable habit, so I tell them the vagaries of everyone's beliefs. The Pope can have as many bottles of wine a day as he likes but the good Moslem is forbidden one drop. On the other hand, the poor Pope cannot have a single wife to aid him and the Moslem can have four. The United Brethren can eat a pig at any time but the Jew must not indulge. We Methodists can swallow anything during January but the devout Moslem must not swallow his own saliva during the fast of Ramadan. I hope I don't end up by teaching the boys to be so tolerant that they think anything goes. I just want them to be good Methodists.

We are going to Shenge to camp when John and Tom come home for the Easter holidays. While looking for camping gear in the warehouse today I found a rarity, a bathtub with a lock and key. I have seen these oval tin tubs with lids since I came to Gbangbama, but I didn't know they came with locks and keys. They were intended for the days of trekking with porters when your bathtub doubled for a trunk or a pantry.

Love, Mama

Dear Lolly and Suzy,

I must be getting old. This is the first April first that I have not played a trick on someone.

We went to Shenge last week and spent three days in the government rest house. In a beautiful leafy bower surrounded by palms, ferns and wild amaryllis, the caretaker had built us a conventional African latrine. He dug a round hole with two, heavy, forked sticks implanted on either side of it. He then laid a sturdy pole across the sticks to form the seat. The final embellishment should have been a pole stuck in the ground in front for the sitter to hold on, but this was omitted.

This tragic oversight brought poor Rob to grief. He was perched, parrot-like, on the pole admiring the scenery one morning when the pole shifted and threw him head over heels into the hole. He was so embarrassed and indignant. I wasn't too happy, either, having to clean up such an apparition before breakfast.

The DC from Moyamba and some guests were staying in an adjoining hut and Rob's disaster brought on a spate of delightful stories. One of the guests had dug his way out of a prisoner-of-war camp during the war by making a tunnel under a latrine. He and his fellow Englishmen could not trust the Frenchmen in the camp with their escape plans, so often a Frenchman would come and sit down above the tunnel-diggers. He said, to make matters worse, the English private who was their lookout, had a face so much like a Frenchman's behind that they were never quite sure what was going on above.

Rob is so glad to have John and Tom home again to resume hostilities. I never see him anymore he is so busy with his brothers and his poultry. He had one hen setting on eleven eggs. The cook told us the kitchen was the place for setting hens and he was right as usual. I set her under the avocado tree and last night we heard the most horrible squawking. We rushed out to find the watchman holding his lantern on the nest, showing a disheveled hen and a coiled cobra. The snake had swallowed ten eggs. Bob shot him and there was great rejoicing and dancing around the corpse. We had seen him twice before around the camp but hadn't been able to catch him. Tom made a poem to commemorate the occasion: "A cobra makes a fowl, Howl."

We have thought of putting hard-boiled eggs in the hen nests to catch the cobras but even a Grinch couldn't be that mean.

Love, Mama

Dear Lolly and Suzy,

We have two little mongooses who look exactly alike. As they are Africans we have named them after the sons of Ham, Cush and Put. Rob is not much of a Bible scholar, so he calls them Push and Cut most of the time.

The seeds enclosed in this letter are calabash seeds for Mother. The ones I sent before will grow gourds the size of dishpans, but these will be as big as bathtubs. The Mendes have gourds and pumpkins growing all over the roofs of their houses. They plant them in the yard and let them run up on the thatched roof where the fruit is safe from goats, children and the majority of bugs.

I am packing boxes to send home. The boys are gathering up things they have collected during this tour: a short elephant tusk, a long python skin and a middle-sized civet-cat hide.

John bought the tusk from a sharp Arab trader and it looks suspiciously like a cow horn to me, but John is happy with it. The python skin is authentic because it is over twenty feet long.

One of the missionaries from Kabala told us a good python story. He was riding along in his rickety truck carrying his rickety pistol when a huge python crossed the road in front of him. His houseboy wanted to run over it but, being a keen hunter, the missionary rejected such crudity. He hopped out of the truck with his pistol in hand but the weapon refused to fire. He frantically worked on it while the houseboy tried to delay the leisurely passage of the reptile. When the head disappeared on one side of the road the boy grabbed the tail as it came out of the bushes on the other side while his master snapped, clicked and shook his unresponsive weapon. The

151

boy clung to the tail and dug in his heels as best he could but the python took little notice, shook him off and glided safely into the bush. Snake fanciers say pythons make the sweetest pets. We have had three small ones at camp which the children wrap around themselves but I don't care for them.

I have been shopping in Freetown trying to buy some clothes for us to wear home. It is a hopeless task. Children don't wear many clothes in Sierra Leone so the stocks are limited, to put it kindly. Some of the things they have for women should be in a museum. The more modern shops offer knickers for sale but I was shown some teddies as well. You will have to ask your grandma what these are. They were out of style even when I was a child.

Love, Mama

Dear Lolly and Suzy,

We have two more new pets, bush babies or galagos. They are relatives of monkeys. They are tiny things with long tails and big round eyes and fur as soft as chinchilla. They normally are tree dwellers and spend their lives jumping from tree to tree. It is startling to see such a small thing jump like a kangaroo. We keep them in the house where they sleep all day and come out to frolic at night, calling to each other in voices like wee sirens. They eat bugs, avocados, bananas and dew. They are so small and eat so little that Bob and I have to get out the magnifying glass to see where they have nibbled off the fruit we put out for them. Bush baby is a good name for them as they look almost human with their expressive eyes and their tiny, human-like hands.

We are getting too many pets; Rob's hen, a mongoose and the civet cat live under the woodpile together in mutual hate and discord. I don't know why one of them doesn't move but they seem to enjoy their quarreling. We are tired of this civet cat. We have loved, fed and protected him all his life and he has never shown us any affection. He comes in the house only to eat and to urinate under the dining-room table. He stalks into the Mess at night, glares at us and waits to be fed. He is getting as big as a dog and I am afraid of him, though he must be a coward since the mongoose chases him all over the woodpile.

The mangoes are ripe and the monkeys and chimpanzees are coming down the mountain to eat them. John, Rob and I eat as fast as we can trying to keep up. Tom is happy for the monkeys to have them as he loathes the fruit. Few people are lukewarm about mangoes, you either love or detest them.

We are planning to go to Paris on the way home, then to Chicago to visit your Aunt Laura. She is my favorite sister since I got this unqualified invitation for all the Spencers to visit her. She said she not only would put out the red carpet, but would buy a new one. I wrote her to hold off buying new carpets until the Spencers had gone.

It is time for me to stop and have a cup of tea. I just found out why the British call tea "char." (After tasting some of it in the Victoria Station restaurant, I thought it was because it was aged in a charred keg.) An English girl told me that "tcha" pronounced char is the Chinese word for tea. She also told me that to have a good cup of tea, you must pour the milk into the cup first. (Everyone uses milk in tea except me.) I am learning the difference between Lapsang, Oolong and Darjeeling teas but I still prefer A & P teabags.

Love, Mama

Dear Lolly and Suzy,

When we were in Freetown we met one of our Greek friends who is just back from leave with a new bride. She is a charming, attractive girl, and they were as happy as could be. It was a marriage arranged by their parents and they had never met until he went home on leave. Arranged marriages are the usual thing among our Greek friends, and I think it is time we tried them in America. So many of our acquaintances are getting divorces that we can't keep up with them from one leave to the next. The more I study the problem, the more I believe that anything as serious and important as marriage should never be based on anything as painful, erratic and mercurial as romantic love. Weddings should be arranged by the sober, benign heads of the families involved. In no other human undertaking except marriage are the ideas of shallow, callow youth allowed to be decisive.

We are so tired of our friends getting divorces because we like them in pairs. We don't know which one to cling to or what to say to either of them. Does one offer congratulations or condolences? Another painful aspect of divorce is that we have to buy twice as many Christmas cards when families split up.

Lolly, you had better plan to go to summer school because I want you to be sure and graduate next year. Your father will sink into despair if he doesn't soon get one child out of school. You have no idea what a tonic it will be for him to see you get your Bachelor of Science degree. The poor man still has such a long way to go. Rob hasn't even started to school yet.

Suzy can meet us in Chicago and drive us home. I will be terrified to drive in all that traffic on the right side of the road or is it the wrong side of the road? I have sent Laura money to buy us a car, a small shooting brake. After riding in European cars, the smallest American car will seem like a bus.

I am having Air France make my reservations in Paris because I want to stay at a very French place. I don't want anyone to know we are Americans so we won't have to spend money. I will let the children's hair grow long like Englishmen and we will all speak Mende.

I have stacks of travel brochures to plan our sightseeing tours. We will visit Versailles, the Louvre, Notre Dame and the Eiffel Tower. Between times we will stroll the boulevards and sip absinthe, whatever that is. We won't frequent the haute-couture salons in our bush costumes. We must save something for another trip.

Love, Mama

GBANGBAMA<br>MAY

Dear Lolly and Suzy,

I am enclosing a headline from the Freetown paper of this week. "I Have Formed a Society to Eat People." This is a direct quote from the defendant according to the police interpreter. Four men are being held for the murder of an eighteen-month-old boy. They used part of his body to make medicine and ate the rest of it. The scene of the murder was near Bonthe and the DC there keeps us informed about the situation. He feels that he may have a small measure of responsibility for the medicine-making.

At Christmas he and a party of Europeans had trouble with their launch offshore from the village that was the scene of the murder. It was dark and they called for someone to come out and send a canoe to Bonthe for aid. No one answered their appeal and the DC finally stormed ashore with his shoes on. This village, as the DC knew, was very strong in the Tun-Tun Society, a secret society of fishermen. No white man is ever supposed to walk in a Tun-Tun village unless he takes off his shoes. As soon as the DC appeared, the natives got very agitated and poured a libation on a pile of stones in the village. The DC was so tired and angry after having been bitten for hours by prime mosquitoes that he paid little attention to the agitation at the time. But now that this murder has been discovered, he is afraid that he may have started the chain of events that led to it.

It is unusual that they have been able to get witnesses and bring the men to trial. It is horrifying to hear how casually they confess now that they have been caught. I guess they see nothing reprehensible in practicing their "religion."

We were up all of last night looking after one of the bush babies. He fell into the chemical toilet and came up covered with the carbolic acid solution. He is only about two inches long if you don't count his tail and when he was wet he looked even smaller. We had an awful time trying to wash him in detergent without killing or drowning him. We spent most of the night washing and warming him, and he seems fine this morning.

We don't know what to do with Rob's baby crocodiles when we come home. I think we will take them up on the mountain and put them in the water-supply tank as a surprise for someone.

The small mongoose has been limping for the past few weeks and a zoologist, wandering through the bush by chance, stopped in and diagnosed his ailment as rickets. He said this was a very common ailment among small animals who have been taken away from their mothers too soon. We have been giving him cod-liver oil, and he is making a dramatic recovery. These frustrating Mendes will drive me stark mad. I just saw Santigi washing the electric iron in a bucket of water, cord and all. Yesterday he told me they were having trouble with the iron. "De iron, it do tremble me! It do pass fire." No wonder it trembled him. It is my fault because I told him to clean it, meaning for him to wipe off the bottom. None of the servants has the slightest fear of the iron, toaster, or electric coffee pot. They operate them daringly and one cannot help admiring their courage since the generator here turns out English electricity which has twice as many volts as the American kind. They experiment ever more dangerously in spite of our trying to watch them all the time. The cook blows up the pressure cooker regularly but he cannot resist having a go at "Na power pot."

Only a few weeks until we come home tra-la tra-la.

Love, Mama

GBANGBAMA
JUNE

Dear Lolly and Suzy,

Have you been reading in the papers about Guinea, Sierra Leone's northern neighbor? She has broken away from France and is now being wooed by Russia. A friend of ours just returned from there and said the place is swarming with Russians, East Germans and Chinese. When Guinea voted to leave the French community of nations, the Frenchmen moved out lock, stock and barrel, even taking the telephones and office furniture with them and destroying all records. Now the Russians have stepped in to give the Guineans aid and comfort. The Russians don't know what they are doing when they

157

try to stir up trouble in Africa. There are enough problems in this continent to stump both the Russians and the Americans for a century.

If anyone can undo the Russians it is the West Africans. Africans are polite, hungry, gay, illiterate, unpredictable rascals. As for their mental capacities, I have devoted every waking moment for four years scheming to outwit even one Mende and I haven't succeeded yet. People say the Africans are like children and I agree wholeheartedly. Who is as full of innocence, pathos and villainy as a child?

Our best clerk has just been sacked for "fiddling the books." (This is English for embezzlement.) Bob sent him down the hill without having him arrested because this takes too much time and effort. In a few minutes he came puffing back up the hill without a speck of shame and said, "Pa, you forgot to write me a recommendation." To think that he was the very rascal who read the Easter lesson so eloquently that I was moved to put two pounds in the collection plate.

Pa and Ma are terms of great respect among the Africans and Bob is always called Pa Spencer when someone seeks a favor. He often gets applications for employment addressed to "Your Lord Worship." The letters here are written in the most flowery Victorian prose by the village letter-writer. For two shillings he will compose a fine letter using his *Letter Writer's Guide* published in 1860. The letters can deal with any aspect of love, death, marriage or money. The writers also specialize in writing forged recommendations for houseboys.

It is time I brought Rob home. This morning I asked him to pick up his wet clothes in the bathroom and he said, "I'm not a servant." I have news for him.

Love, Mama

Dear Lolly and Suzy,

I am curing a leopard skin with the aid of a book entitled *Easy Home Tanning.* Of all the lying, ambiguous, misleading titles I have ever read, this one is tops. The skin is a fine fresh one that the village hunters brought your father and it is eight feet long from nose to tail. When it is wet it feels as though it weighs a ton. The skin must be scraped and dipped in a solution of sulphuric acid, soft soap, borax and water, then scraped and dipped again and again. For three days I have been staggering back and forth with the pelt, from sink, to barrel, to table, surrounded by clouds of green flies and the curses of the other Europeans at camp. The whole venture is Bob's idea. He is sure I can tan a skin if I put my mind to it. What degradation people will endure for flattery. When tanning a pelt, one must be particularly careful not to damage the whiskers or the eye holes or the nose holes. I am so tired and discouraged that I have thought of suicide but it would be so unfair to the old leopard to give up now. The skin just steams and stinks. There must be better tanning weather than this—yesterday we had six inches of rain.

We are all packed and ready to come home as soon as the boys are out of school. Where shall we live, Alabama or Florida? I wish we were coming home for good to settle down at Bugtussle among the Jukes and Kallikaks of North Florida and live happily ever after.

The boys and I will stay about six months—long enough for them to have one term of American school. Your father will come home in September and stay for two months. We hate to be away from Sierra Leone next fall when the Queen is coming for a visit.

You can't believe the upheaval that a country goes through

for a royal visit. In this small, poor country I don't know why things can't be left in their natural state. Sierra Leone's chief appeal is that it is so startlingly different from a modern country, yet everyone is knocking himself out to get a thin veneer of modernity over everything before the Queen comes.

I just walked out to my lettuce patch and the garden boy stood there urinating on the compost heap. He said, "Good afternoon," and calmly continued his performance. That is savoir faire. Bob says that Africans urinate when they want to be nonchalant, the way we would yawn or stretch or smooth our hair. Drivers are being trained for the Queen's visit—not to drive but to refrain from urinating in her presence. They are certainly not burdened by our Puritan modesty. Your father and brothers are getting pretty casual about this themselves. We will have to look sharp or they will disgrace us in civilization.

Love, Mama

PARIS
JUNE

Dear Lolly,

I will write you a note from Paris since you are in school and won't be able to meet us in Chicago.

We are staying on the Quai d'Orsay in a nice old French hotel with a bathtub big enough for the whole family. Once they do decide to install plumbing, these Europeans are no slouches.

The Seine is flowing right outside our windows and just across the river is the Louvre. Within walking distance on my left is the Eiffel Tower and on my right is Notre Dame. Everything is exactly where it should be. I love Paris in spite of its being full of Frenchmen. I used to think Frenchmen

160

didn't like me but now I have met enough to realize that there is nothing personal involved; they simply don't like anybody, especially other Frenchmen.

The boys have enjoyed sightseeing up to now but I mustn't push them too far—museum-tramping is not to their tastes. They love hanging about on the Eiffel Tower but the lopsided elevator makes me seasick. John and Tom were impressed with the obelisk in the Place de la Concorde when I told them that Moses had seen it when he led the Children of Israel out of the land of Egypt. I am not positive that he did but I don't think anyone can check.

I must go and help Tom get his money changed. We stopped in Madrid and he had his English money changed into pesetas to buy a carved bull. The minute we arrive at an airport he rushes up and converts his money. We were late getting into Orly, so he didn't have time to deal with the money changers last night, and now he is fuming because the hotel clerk is cool toward changing fifty-cents worth of pesetas into francs.

Tom left Freetown with an infected navel with pink, concentric rings around it like the rings of Saturn. The doctor told me to watch it carefully as he had excised (cut out) the navels of six European patients since he had been in Sierra Leone. It is some kind of fungus infection. It looks much better today, thank heaven. I had visions of a prolonged stay in Paris to have a navel excised.

I will see you in less than a week. Aunt Laura wants us to visit in Chicago for a while, but I think we will take her to Alabama with us instead. I can't wait to get home—peaches, watermelons, sweet corn and you!

Love, Mama

# Tour III: 1960-1961

Dear Lolly and Suzy,

Here we are in mid-Atlantic, on our way back to the bush. I have traveled this route so often that it doesn't seem so far from home now. Why is it so much easier to get *to* the bush than *from* the bush? We rode on a jet plane from Atlanta to New York that went faster on the ground than the plane we left Freetown on went in the air.

As soon as I got aboard this plane for Dakar the steward came up and gave me a note from your father. He had been on this same plane three days before when it left Johannesburg for New York. He got off in West Africa and sent this note on to me as he thought I would be returning to Africa in this plane. That is real service by Pan American to deliver a little scrap of paper by hand from so far. Bob had come to Johannesburg via San Francisco and Australia. He had to go the opposite way around the world to Africa on urgent business, so he said. Some people will go to any extreme to avoid travel with children.

The little ones have been reasonably good. A blizzard was raging in New York and they played outside in the snow for half-minute intervals while we waited for our plane. The rest of the time they spent checking phone booths for abandoned dimes and squatting around various newsstands reading comics for free. I planned to do some Christmas shopping after we were all weighed in but the shops in the airport had such junk at such exorbitant prices that I didn't buy anything. So many foreigners come through Idlewild that the State Department should see that the shops sell things that are representative of the joys of capitalism. The shoddy goods reminded me of the tourist traps that we set for rich Yankees in Florida.

Bob will be in Freetown when we arrive and he should have the Christmas boxes unpacked. I sent them in October and I hope he has Santa Claus all ready because we won't get to Gbangbama until Christmas Eve.

I am forty years old today and I feel so young. I don't mind being forty. I would hate to be your age again. You are so tender and so vulnerable to the cruel blows of the world. I am tough and insulated and getting more insulated by the minute as I stuff down all the good food on this plane. This will be our last chance until our next leave. Pass me another glass of milk.

Love, Mama

GBANGBAMA<br>CHRISTMAS

Dear Lolly and Suzy,

It is the small frustrations in Africa that are the final straw and make me want to weep with homesickness. Do you realize that I have been keeping house all the time I have been here without a decent broom or can opener? The English have no equivalent of an American broom. Their brooms are either heavy like those that street sweepers use or soft as velvet with bristles like water-color brushes. The Mendes have a good short broom made of piassava fiber which is like our brooms but it is next to impossible to find one to buy. Every time I get back to Africa, I vow that the next time I board an airliner in New York, I will be carrying a broom but when I am home, my passion for proper sweeping dims and I come back without one. A broom is such an embarrassing piece of luggage.

I did bring a good wall opener back with me on my first leave but it was useless. All English and European cans have a different sized rim and only one can in a dozen would open with my opener.

The Canadian and the two Australians had the Christmas tree up and three turkeys in the freezer, so we will have a festive holiday. Bob brought me some beautiful pearls from Australia, but since there is no one to show them to, I don't really care about them. Ladies want presents only to show to other ladies. The boys got boxing gloves and have been sparring around all day—nothing new about this except the gloves.

Everybody at camp was glad to see us because they need a fourth for bridge. One of the Australians has gone on leave and they have been reduced to using the chimpanzee for a fourth.

I brought the steward boys pictures of themselves that I had developed in America. They look at the picture upside-down until you show them the right way. I have looked at pictures from the day I was born so it seems incredible to me that a bushman can't understand perspective. Most of our house-boys had never seen a picture or a book until we came. Sometimes when they are dusting they will often hang the picture back upside-down. Bob bought some material printed with large African scenes—canoes, thatched huts and palm trees, and took them to the tailor to have shirts made. You would think they would recognize pictures of their own scenery but the tailor made the shirts with all the pattern upside-down. Bob could not explain to him why he was not pleased. He thought Bob was complaining about the sewing and kept saying, "Na fine buttonhole, Pa."

I see that the Africans are planning protests against the French who plan to set off an atomic device in the Sahara.

Lolly, doesn't studying genetics make you want to kick all the generals of the world in the teeth? Men are impossible. Just now John and Rob are running around shooting cap guns at each other while Tom is studiously drawing a huge trailer which is towing a guided missile. Women spend their time thinking of self-preservation rather than self-destruction. Only today I have been using royal-bee jelly on my recalcitrant double chins. Aunt Ruth gave me this jar. She has abandoned bee jelly and gone on to something more modern and expensive. But the idea is the important thing. Preservation instead of destruction.

I remember learning when I was a little girl that atoms were too small to be divided. I wish it were true. We got along fine just changing molecules.

Lolly, I was interested in your inviting Tommy's mother out to Grandma's house for a family dinner. This looks serious.

Love, Mama

GBANGBAMA<br>JANUARY

Dear Lolly and Suzy,

Your father is so happy today that his faith in mankind is boundless. His wallet containing nine pounds has been lost and returned with all the money intact. It fell out of his pocket yesterday when he got out of the Land Rover at Momaligi and one of his laborers brought it back today.

We went to Bonthe today and found there had been a complete changeover of Europeans. Everyone we knew there is gone and this set of inhabitants is completely nuts. One of them believes in reincarnation and another rides up and down the promenade on a bicycle, clad only in his shirt. We were

168

glad to get back to Gbangbama and our own brand of crockery.

The men who were caught for the Tun-Tun Society murder near Bonthe were hanged while we were on leave. Several of the village elders were taken to Freetown to witness the execution so they could take a true account back to the village. At the hanging, one by one, the hood was lifted from the heads of the murderers so the witnesses could see them. We know the European doctor who was in attendance and he said it was a horrible affair.

The boys have gone back to school and I miss them terribly. I am so irritable and mean I detest everybody and the harmattan and the mongoose. It broke my heart to send Rob off, but Bob said he must go. Of course Rob wanted to go and hasn't missed me an instant. But what can I do with no children? I have had so many for so long.

I must go and feed the old tomcat. I never cared for him before, but now he reminds me of Rob and I get a vague comfort from being near him. I hope John will make Rob wash his ears and teeth. Lolly, here is a sobering thought to make you frugal. The Spencers have approximately two hundred and twenty-four teeth to be cleaned, filled and cared for.

Love, Mama

Dear Lolly and Suzy,

This is a sad quiet day for Gbangbama as Kpana Bum, the Paramount Chief, is dead. He died on the way home from Freetown where he had been to visit the Premier. Last week the chief asked for a vehicle to take him to Freetown as the

169

Premier had sent for him. He got sick while there and sent for two of his wives to come and nurse him. Early this morning a government ambulance arrived with his body. He was sent home while he was dying because it would have been impolitic for the Premier to have a paramount chief die in his compound. Besides, Kpana Bum would have wanted to die in his own village.

Just now his body is lying on his bed in the sacred bush, a grove of large trees near the village, but there is great palaver between the pagan and Christian factions in the village as to what kind of burial he will have. The Chief was baptized in the village church last month. The African pastor is a fine old man, respected by Christian and pagan alike, so he may have his way, although the missionaries say they have never known of a paramount chief in this part of the country to have a Christian burial.

A delegation has just come up from the village to borrow nails and boards, so they must be going to make a coffin. In pagan rites the body is simply wrapped in a white cloth. Maybe we will be invited to the funeral. If he is buried in the bush, women won't be allowed to go near. Nurse Bard had to detour about ten miles to get home today because the road goes through the sacred bush and she wasn't allowed to drive by.

One of the houseboys is a member of the Temne tribe, and he told us that when a Temne chief died, his head was cut off and saved to bury with the body of the next chief. Then his body was buried with the head they had kept from the previous chief, assuring continuity of line. I wonder where they keep the head.

Love, Mama

Dear Lolly and Suzy,

The Christian faction won the decision to bury the chief and the Roses and Spencers were invited to the funeral. Joan and I keep our only hats in Freetown, so we hurriedly made chapeaux out of scarves and sun hats. Bob and Bill wore their coats throughout the ninety-degree afternoon.

The program was a fascinating blend of pagan and Christian rites. We walked along the hot, dusty road, following the coffin from Kpana Bum's house to the church. A Land Rover had been borrowed for a hearse and was followed by six court messengers and ten or twelve of his wives. As we walked along a man beside the coffin blew a soft, mournful dirge on a carved elephant tusk. We all sang in Mende, "Jesus, Lover of My Soul, Let Me to Thy Bosom Fly." It was a long walk and we sang it over and over. The wives and sisters sat on the front benches of the church, naked from the waist up, their skin smeared with ashes. Their lappas were pitifully ragged as this is the proper apparel for mourning. The pastor preached a fine sermon, taking advantage of this unusually full house to make sinners sit up and take note. He told how the chief had sought Christ in his final months on earth and how he had served his people well and had lived up to his name of Peacemaker. The sermon was very moving and I wept unashamedly, whether for Kpana Bum or for the frailty of man, I can't say.

We sat up front close to the coffin, and it was apparent that the corpse was thirty-six hours old. (There is no embalming in Sierra Leone.) There was a coffee grove nearby which was in bloom and every now and then the sweet fragrance of the coffee blossoms gave a pleasant change to the air.

After the sermon we followed the body to the graveside

171

singing "Onward Christian Soldiers" accompanied by the mournful horn. While we were at the grave two half-naked pagan wives came shrieking out of the bush and threw themselves on the ground and screamed and rolled in the dust—billowing clouds of it. All of a sudden there was a tremendous *boom* of a cannon which nearly made me jump out of my skin. I knew there was an old cannon around but I thought it was defunct. Bob was near enough to see the second blast which was fired after the funeral. He said the villagers stood the weapon on end, packed it with leaves, dynamite, and dirt, then tied it to a tree with vines, dropped a lighted faggot to the powder train and ran like hell. This profanity is your father's. (He ran like hell too.) I was on the other side of the crowd and was ignorant of the second blast, too, so again I jumped about six feet in the air and passed your father on the homestretch.

It will be several months at least before another chief is chosen—one who could possibly be a woman. The African's affection is always for his mother and his sisters in preference to his wives or children, a nephew being more likely to succeed a chief than his son. This is a sensible aspect of African culture. There are a lot more perfidious wives throughout history than there are perfidious mothers and sisters.

Lolly, your letters are overflowing with plans—plans for graduation and plans for getting married. Slow up. You simply can't get married until we come home and I don't know when that will be as Bob is very busy. I know you have plenty of grandmas and aunts to marry you off but you just can't get married without me. I won't be done out of the blue lace I always planned to wear.

Love, Mama

Dear Lolly and Suzy,

The houseboy is shelling peanuts today and when he shells he gets loquacious and tells me lots of news and answers lots of questions. He told me that some woman dropped dead in the village last night because she "dun witch hersef." He meant that she was full of such strong witch power that it ate her up. He also explained to me why Mendes don't like twins. A woman who has twins is believed to have trod the primrose path with a spirit, so twins are half spirit and half human. Twin babies used to be killed but that custom is dying out.

Abu killed a green mamba this morning which was sunning itself in the orange tree. I worry twice as much about snakes here as I do at Bugtussle because African snakes are so unpredictable. In Florida the moccasins, coral and rattlesnakes all stay on the ground but here the poison snakes are just as much at home in the top of a tree. The colors of the African snakes are as deceitful as their habitats. The mamba is the color of our harmless grass snake and the cobra looks like our black racer—until he gets angry. Then he spreads his wide hood and spits his venom accurately from six to eight feet. The venom is aimed at the eye of the prey to cause blindness, then the snake can kill you with a conventional bite. Rob's little roommate in Kabala opened his drawer and a cobra was curled up on his socks. The snake spit in the little boy's eye but the school nurse washed it out immediately and no permanent damage was done. Rob is so proud to know someone a cobra spit on, and there was glory for John, too, as he shot the snake with his .22. I'll bet there are no boarding schools in America with cobras in the dressers.

The ugliest snake in Sierra Leone is the Gaboon viper which

is also the largest poisonous snake in Africa. They are seldom over five feet long but their thickness makes them very heavy. We have a skin from one killed near here that is five feet two inches long. It was so fat, thick and ugly that it made me sick. These snakes can give birth to as many as fifty offspring at once, each fully armed and ready to make his first kill. This kind of viper can puff himself up and deflate with a noise as loud as a tractor blowout. For me the snake could save his venom—a reptilian raspberry that loud would scare me to death.

Some loofah seeds are enclosed in this letter. A loofah is a gourd the size of a large cucumber that dries with a tough fibrous center. It is the bushman's bath sponge and steel wool. I use it as the base of a French hair roll.

Lolly, your father was so happy to get your sensible letter. Why don't you make him happy more often by discussing your plans for employment? I don't blame him for being overjoyed at the prospect of exchanging a consumer for a wage earner. There are so many consumers in the Spencer household.

Love, Mama

GBANGBAMA<br>APRIL

Dear Lolly and Suzy,

Lolly, I must bow to superior strength of will and enter into the wedding plans. I feel so ineffectual from several thousand miles away. You must have a simple wedding with Suzy for your only attendant. Your Grandpa Spencer or Cousin Berney can give you away. In spite of all the forces you have mobilized, I keep hoping that you can't possibly get married without me. But then I thought Rob could never leave me at such a tender age and go to boarding school, and the little wretch has never looked back. Woe, woe.

We were almost eaten alive by driver ants last night. At least they are reputedly able to eat anything as big as an elephant. The largest things I have known them to kill are puppies, kittens and hens.

We played bridge until about ten thirty, then came down to our house and went straight to sleep without an ant in sight. A little after eleven I was awakened for some reason, feeling afraid. There was a faint rustle around the room. I shook Pa and said, "Get up. I'm frightened." He groaned at the perversity of women, opened one eye and turned on the flashlight beside the bed. Then he jumped straight across the room, turned on the wall switch and leaped back into bed, touching the floor only once. The light revealed a thick carpet of pulsating ants, millions of them. The rustle I had heard was from all the peaceable beetles and geckos trying to get away from the ants. So far, there were none on the bed, but in the half hour we had been asleep, they had completely covered every room in the house. They came in under the doors and windows and there were great wads of them as big as tennis balls near the doors. Bob and I stood up in bed, looked at each other, looked at the invaders and decided to flee. With a few broad jumps we were out of the house and up the hill to the guesthouse where we spent the night. We got a good many bites on our feet but considered ourselves lucky. Returning home by daylight in our scanty attire presented a ticklish problem, but we arrived to find all the ants gone and the house clean as a pin.

Ants always travel at night or in the shade as they hate sun and a few minutes' exposure to bright sun will kill them. If it is necessary for them to travel in the sun, they build little tunnels of clay on top of the ground to protect them. It is useful to know that they hate sun. I used to spend hours picking little ants out of the sugar bag. Now I just put it in a pan in the sun and they are gone in a jiffy.

Driver ants are made up of soldiers and workers, the former being twice as big and as mean as the workers. When they are marching, the soldiers form two columns on the outside to protect the workers in the center who move faster than the soldiers. Every few minutes some of the soldiers leave the column, circle out for a few feet, stand on their hind legs and wave their pinchers in the air looking for something to bite. They have a vicious bite and it takes a hard tug to get them off. Each bite gouges out a piece of flesh and leaves a drop of blood so it is easy to see how they could devour an animal. They eat nothing but flesh and all are completely blind.

I have been watching the little critters all the time I have been in Africa but I never really had a personal interest in them until last night. I have almost got Bob to admit that there is an imbalance of ants in Africa.

Love, Mama

GBANGBAMA
MAY

Dear Lolly and Suzy,

I have said that Africans carry everything on their heads but I didn't know that included corpses. Bill Rose was walking in the bush yesterday and passed a convoy of two half-naked Mendes trotting down the path with a homemade stretcher on their heads. Wrapped in a mat and lashed to the stretcher was a body with two white feet sticking out. Thinking it might be someone he knew (one is prepared for anything here), Bill rushed up for a closer look but the legs were black so he went on his way. In life Africans have pink soles on their feet and, in death, they are as white as mine.

I cleaned out the record cabinet this morning and gave Luceni some old 78-rpm records. Now instead of "Back to Back and Belly to Belly" drifting up from the village, I hear Dimitri Mitropoulos conducting Chopin's Concerto No. 1 in E Minor. I'll bet the Minneapolis Symphony Orchestra never expected to play in Gbangbama.

We spend all of our time at camp discussing the approaching wedding. I hope Lolly and Tommy don't get so tired and harassed that they decide to elope after all the work and planning the aunts have done to make a perfect wedding.

We had a letter from John today and his roommate's father has invited him to go on an elephant hunt near Bintemani, Sierra Leone's highest mountain. We were all invited to go but Bob says I could never walk forty miles and then climb seven thousand feet. Imagine our little John going elephant hunting—and with a pellet gun, the right caliber for butterflies. It is really just a hiking trip but it is possible for them to see elephant, deer and wild boar in that part of the country. In the seventeenth century Sierra Leone had the finest elephant "teeth" in all of Africa. Surely there will be one left for John.

I have been reading of the sit-in strikes of the Negro students in America. If only Americans knew how avidly everything that happens there is reported in the world press. Little Rock, Montgomery and Tuscaloosa are familiar names in Asia and Africa. I hope I can teach you young Spencers to fight the Klansmen and their ilk with all your strength. Don't become enamored of your white skin. It is a poor measuring rod for worth. Use brain or heart or backbone if you must measure by anatomy.

Suzy, thanks for sending the shoebox full of my African letters. You are sweet to think that I can write a book from them. You know how despondent I have been with all my children gone and now you have opened up a new world for me. Fame, fortune and a career! My only talent heretofore has been for washing diapers but I will try something else. It is only two months until I come on leave and if I am busy on my book, the time will fly.

Love, Mama

# Tour IV: 1961-1962

Dear Lolly and Suzy,

Here we are starting our fourth tour of Africa, leaving three children in the New World. It broke my heart to leave John because he prefers Africa to Alabama but he is too old for the school in Kabala.

The monotony of the same old flight across the Atlantic was relieved this time because your father traveled first class and Tom, Rob and I traveled on the return half of our tourist tickets. I usually go tourist because one can meet nicer people —poets, housewives, students and missionaries—and go twice as far for the same amount of money. Bob never practices these plebeian economies because he is always in a hurry and has seen enough countries and people.

When we got on the plane in New York the passengers glared at him while he sheepishly carried in the accordion, baseball bat and umbrella, and settled his poor wife and children in the tourist compartment then hurriedly retired to the Presidential Suite. Rob, suffering the stigma of segregation, squatted in the aisle and peered through the crack in the curtain at the glittering world of privilege. After our adequate but uninspiring dinner Tom attempted to stir up class consciousness by darting in and bringing back Bob's menu, a parchment sheet the size of a large calendar. I read aloud the list of opulent courses while the discontented masses listened. There was *La Perdrix des Neiges du Tibet avec Riz Sauvage* and *Le Ris de Veau Financiers*. Roughly this is Himalayan Quail with Savage Rice and Financier's Sweetbreads.

One of the nice things about being in Africa is that you have to go through Europe to get here. We had a nice visit in London with your Aunt Ruth who has a flat in Kensington. This is a good part of town, with Princess Margaret and the Russian ambassador living up the road. I am lucky to have five sisters. That our visits can be diluted among five households is the only thing that makes them possible.

The weather was perfect and Ruth and I left the boys at the zoo looking at West African snakes and took a bus to tour the countryside. Because of the beautiful day traffic was terrible. England should ban automobiles before it is too late. There is simply not room for them.

Flowers were blooming everywhere with a dazzling brilliance. Even the smallest dwelling has a scrap of garden or at least a window box. It is said if there is one Englishman anywhere in the world there will be a garden and if there are two, there will be a club. I was surprised to see so many semitropical plants in England. Camellias and azaleas thrive even though it is farther north than Newfoundland. The length of the days makes one realize how far north Britain is. It is possible to take pictures at ten o'clock at night.

We took the boys sightseeing around London the next day but unless I kindled their interest with gory tales, they were as stubborn as mules about going. They were bored with Westminster Abbey until I explained that it was full of dead bodies. They plodded around Whitehall with me for hours looking for the place where Charles I lost his head. I confided that head-chopping was absolutely de rigueur in the Tower of London and they went without protest. The Bloody Tower where small Prince Edward and his brother were smothered enchanted them. Wandering through the Tower I felt a momentary pang of sadness for the dull life that royalty has been forced into nowadays.

We went to Windsor Castle which is on a hill overlooking the Thames. The village of Stoke Poges is in sight across the fields. This was the scene of Gray's village churchyard where he wrote the immortal words which I have often muttered under my breath while living in some miserable mining camp. "Full many a flower is born to blush unseen, and waste its sweetness on the desert air."

From London we flew to Paris for a short stopover. We shopped around the airport but there was nothing to buy but intoxicating spirits and perfume. The spirits were cheaper, ounce for ounce, so we bought spirits. In a moment of exhibitionism I asked Bob to buy a bottle of Green Chartreuse because I had read that it was the most expensive drink in the world. I never meant him to buy it but he did. It tastes horrible. Well, I can always use it to take off nail polish.

We had a miserable flight from Paris via a certain Gallic airline whose name I will not let pass my lips. People fly with them only because their food is good—when they feed you. After a crowded overnight flight from Paris we were treated to hard rolls and coffee at 6:00 A.M. and then didn't get another bit until we arrived in Freetown at 6:00 P.M. We left Dakar on something like a DC-1 and it took us twelve hours to travel five hundred miles. We stopped at every camel track so most of the time was spent on the ground. We flew low and the weather was stormy so everyone was airsick. Rob wouldn't relinquish his vomit bag even when we landed at the various places. He would stagger off the plane clutching it desperately while the stewardess tried to snatch it from him. Even in his weakened condition he managed to outwit her each time.

We stopped at a place I had never been, Ziganchor. I don't

know what country it was in as there was nothing to give me a clue. Several villainous-looking Europeans of the criminal type and a few Africans were about but they and the plane crew were all speaking different languages, none of which I understood. However, new places and experiences always give my spirits a lift so I will always remember Ziganchor with the same warm feeling I experienced when I was bitten by a wombat.

The temperature on the plane was ninety degrees even at eight thousand feet. This mystery was solved when three hundred baby chickens got off with us in Freetown. People can stand ninety degrees but chicks cannot survive a chill so the fowl were favored. Your father says cargo is more important in Africa than passengers.

Write. Write. Write. When I think of leaving you all I feel such a stab of pain that I know my heart must break. But then I remember how healthy, beautiful, rich and blessed I am and I strive on.

Love, Mama

Dear Lolly and Suzy,

Bob has had a few days' work to do in Freetown so we haven't gone up to the bush yet.

Lolly, I hope I haven't made a mistake in persuading you and Tommy to give up your apartment and take a house with Suzy and John. If you all live together you can afford a nicer place and I will be so much happier if you are all in the same nest. I selfishly want a home for John and haven't considered you and Tommy and Suzy too much. You are all such agreeable people individually that I trust you won't detest living with each other. When Tom is too old for the school in Kabala I will put him and John in boarding school but I couldn't send John off to an institution all alone.

Freetown looks much the same since Sierra Leone acquired its independence from England. During the independence celebrations all the government opposition was either jailed or absorbed into the ruling party so there would be no danger of embarrassing situations while foreign visitors were in the country. Now the opposition has been freed and things have returned to normal with the politicians pouring out invective, libel and slander on the heads of the people they are most friendly with outside the realm of politics. The problems of Sierra Leone are staggering but there are able men of goodwill in power and I believe they can keep the country stable.

There are many new Americans in Sierra Leone: an ambassador, several aid missions and fifty Peace Corps teachers. They are all so eager to help and understand Africa. From my lofty perch of a few years' experience, I want to warn them not to take any wooden nickels. I believe only Africans can help other Africans. I think American money should be spent only for education. I am a great booster for Peace Corps teachers. A crash program to develop every possible native teacher to send into the primary schools is the only way to bring Sierra Leone into the twentieth century. Africans smile and say "Yes" when they are told or even showed how to conserve their land, feed their people or save their babies, then when the teller's back is turned the Africans go back to their way of doing things. Before people will change their way of life they must understand the reasons for doing so. Nobody can be told anything. This is a universal human trait and there is no evidence that the African lacks it.

Every week a highly qualified mission nurse, trained in midwifery at Johns Hopkins, comes to Gbangbama. Her sole interest is mothers and babies but she hardly gets enough patients to justify her maternity clinic. When the mother is dying of puerperal fever or the baby is having convulsions from tetanus (very common, from cutting the cord with a filthy knife) the family will graciously let the nurse have a go with her kind of medicine. But not until they have tried all the Mende treatments.

CARE is sponsoring a free-lunch program for the schools in Sierra Leone, using surplus foods donated by the United States. To qualify for the food the school must have a safe place to store it and have mothers prepare a place to cook it. (This involves a large iron pot set on three stones.) Before I went on leave I told the village elders and the schoolmaster about the program, explained how to get in touch with CARE, and offered our warehouse as a storage place for the food. Naturally when I came back after seven months I expected the Gbangbama school to be serving free lunches. But they are doing nothing of the kind. I did hear that Kabati is using the program and I was thrilled beyond measure at the progress of my old hometown.

Why the African wants the mixed blessings of the twentieth century takes some thought but if he does he must learn the rules and regulations. The only place to learn them is at school.

I am a little behind in the twentieth century myself. I was always going to sit down and figure out how a telephone worked. Then the radio came along and radar and television and nuclear fission and space travel and I still don't understand the telephone. I can never catch up now. I had better find a few reactionary Mendes who don't want the twentieth century, then I'll go back and join them.

Bob took us out for dinner last night at Freetown's new hotel. It is certainly in the twentieth century and the food and service were excellent. If I were an American tourist I would come to Sierra Leone for a holiday. The hotel is first class now and the beaches and scenery always have been.

Love, Mama

Dear Lolly and Suzy,

We have arrived at camp in the middle of a record rainy season, forty inches last month and seven inches today. Statistics are meaningless to anyone except a meteorologist but this means that it is darned wet. There is a bumper crop of mushrooms growing in the kitchen and snails are flourishing everywhere. I even found one in my bed last night. It was really a slug as proper snails have shells. We have that kind in the garden with shells as big as grapefruit.

I am becoming a scatologist of note around Gbangbama. Roughly, scatology is the study of turds or scats. I just discovered the word scatology a few weeks ago when reading one of the children's nature books but I have been a student of the science for years. Our house here is so full of scats every morning that it is useful to know whether they belong to a snake, a cockroach, a lizard or a bush cat.

The rain drove thousands of things into the house while we were on leave. Cocoons are hanging from the ceilings like stalactites, all shapes and colors, with a splendid variety of things inside: worms, spiders, moths and millipedes. Many improvident bugs have just pasted their eggs on the walls without cocoons. Every drawer is full of things which I took to be mothballs but Tom says they are lizard eggs. Nurse Bard is on leave now and the new nurse came last week and carefully gathered up the pills that she thought someone had

187

spilled. She discarded them when they began to hatch little lizards.

The tree outside the house is covered with caterpillars who keep crawling under the door. I will tether the rooster outside and he will make quick work of them.

The bush adjoining camp has been cleared for rice farms this year and all the snakes who lived there have come to us for resettlement. We have never had so many. I am beginning to look at my cherished shrubs and trees through African eyes and to see them solely as a hiding place for snakes.

One of the ladies at camp was tidying up her bedroom and a large green mamba fell out of the ceiling at her feet. He had crawled in through the ventilator. Luckily the fall stunned him and she was able to escape. This is the same house where Suzy found one curled up in the bathroom last year. I'll never forget how she calmly came out of the house like an Atlas rocket.

Some ignoramus in Freetown told me that there were no mambas in Sierra Leone but when the garden boy killed this one yesterday I consulted Bob's snake book and found that it was a Hallowell green mamba with the thirteen prescribed rows of scales around his belly. Rob found a Traill's green mamba with the nineteen prescribed rows of scales. I always keep a copy of Cansdale's *Reptiles of West Africa* on my bedside table to read at night. It helps me unwind.

The children want a python for a pet. They say that it is the friendliest of all snakes and the most responsible. Most snakes go off willy-nilly and leave their eggs to hatch themselves but the African python hatches hers like a hen, curled around them for six weeks. The eggs are as large as oranges and there can be as many as fifty in a clutch. There is a small python in Sierra Leone who is so shy he rolls himself into a ball and hides his face when molested. The Mendes call him a "shame" snake.

There is also a clever egg-eating snake here who eats the eggs and spits out the shells. When the egg gets in the back of his throat his ribs contract and break it, letting the egg slip down and the shell come out.

People are more afraid of snakes than they should be. Last night we were playing bridge in the Mess and a long, slender one came crawling in. We jumped up and clubbed him to death with our umbrellas only to find that he was a harmless file snake whose diet is made up solely of other snakes. The delightful story of the Agricultural Officer's wife in Njala is a perfect illustration of snake panic. She went into her two-holer privy one morning for some fruitful meditation, sat down, then jumped to her feet screaming, "I've been bitten by a snake!" Her husband, an efficient boy scout type, quickly took command of the situation, noted the ominous punctures on her ample behind, and slashed them with a razor to remove the poison. After she was treated and soothed a posse was organized to capture the snake. They went into the privy armed with sticks and guns, looked into the hole and found a large Rhode Island Red hen.

Snakes or no, I am glad to be home. I have been here long enough now that I think of Gbangbama as home. After all, there is not much of a transition from Alabama to Gbangbama. When I was in the States I caught myself saying several times, "When I go home I am going to do thus and so."

Love, Mama

Dear Lolly and Suzy,

We were horrified at the .22 rifle ejecting debris in John's eye, and more horrified that the little rascal didn't tell you until next day. Thank heaven the doctor says it will be all right. John knows the ladies in our family hate guns and I suppose he didn't want any I-told-you-so's from his sisters. But he knows his father is on his side and thinks all boys should be Nimrods. Anyway you must impress on him that his eyes are so precious he must confess any injury to them even if he gets the injury while filing his way into the First National Bank.

I will write a short letter today as I have many household duties which call. Every week or so I find it necessary to have a tantrum for the benefit of the staff. I dive into dresser drawers, rip open closet doors and kitchen cabinets, rant and wave my arms and shout, "Where is my whatchamacallit?" This performance strikes fear into uneasy consciences and all the servants think that I have missed what they have stolen. An astonishing number of things appear which I had forgotten I owned. Also our consumption of sugar and fat is cut in half for a few days until the memory of my tantrum grows dim.

Your father engaged a French chef when I went on leave and I cannot get rid of him. He is a Guinean who came to Sierra Leone when his French master left Guinea. Bob has an absurd loyalty to him because he speaks French, but with my twenty years around the kitchen, I know that he has never been anything more than a serving boy. Because he calls coffee "café" and cheese "fromage," Bob is willing to overlook almost any amount of gross malpractice around the stove. Momodu simply can't cook. Rob has taught him to make pancakes but we can't go on eating crepes suzette for a whole tour. That is, nobody could except Rob. Luckily Tom is getting tired of pancakes so he is ready to help me give Momodu the heave-ho.

Bob says that I am just hard to please which isn't true. I am a most lenient housekeeper. (Downright slovenly, some call it.) The only excessive demand which I make on the servants is that they respect and preserve the little piles of seeds which I collect and leave lying around on the sink, dresser, typewriter, stove and radio. Your father, not I, sacked both previous cooks, Kamara because he smoked hashish and Ansumana because he stole Bob's toenail clippers. I know Ansumana meant to return the clippers but was just unfortunate enough to be having a pedicure on the same day that Bob needed one.

Love, Mama

GBANGBAMA<br>OCTOBER

Dear Lolly and Suzy,

The Queen is coming to Sierra Leone and I hope that I can see her. I have seen a platypus, a buffalo and a whooping crane and I would like to add a queen to my list of rare and diminishing species.

All the people in the bush are practicing their dances for the durbar to be held in her honor at Bo. Durbar is a word which the British have brought to Africa from India. It means celebration.

A nearby village invited us to see their star dancer practice and we drove over a tooth-shaking bush track about twenty miles to see him. It was worth the trip as he was very good, leaping through hoops, dancing on broken glass and doing spinning leaps from a homemade trampoline. What made his exhibit so remarkable was that he depended on casual labor to

191

help with his act. He would exhort his audience to come forward and hold the hoops or the trampoline but they would hang back, chew their cola nuts and look shyly at their feet. He would shout and entreat and finally drag them bodily to his aid. It is no wonder that they were reluctant. To improvise a trampoline out of a fishing net and hold it taut enough to bounce a man twenty feet in the air is hard work. Each time the dancer came down from a leap I expected the circle of men holding the net to cave in but the dancer would roll out a string of invective to straighten their backs. It was extraordinary how he could be stage director and star at the same time. He finally got two men to hold some hoops at just the right angle for him to make a flying leap through them. The drums were beating frenziedly and he was poised, ready to take off when a mangy mongrel wandered between the hoop-bearers and broke the spell. Everything stopped while the whole village beat the feckless pup.

Ggangbama, too, has been practicing for the Queen and last night they continued throughout the night because the moon was full. How they knew it was full is a mystery; it rained most of the night and the sky was as black as pitch. The Mendes always know what the moon is doing whether they can see it or not. A few of them should be sent to Canaveral as consultants because their moon sensitivity is much further developed than ours.

Lately I am getting interested in going to the moon. The more Bob tells me about it, the more reasonable it sounds. The moon will make a perfect base for exploring the rest of the universe since it has no gravity and heavy space vehicles can be launched with little trouble. Too, there is no atmosphere and no weather—a huge vacuum. Scientists like vacuums for some reason, the bigger the better. If a little vacuum tube is so wonderful, just think how valuable miles of vacuum must be.

However I find the prospect of no weather unsettling. I love weather. Life would be grim with no summer days or spring breezes or winter storms. Weather has a profound effect on one's mood, so care must be taken to launch the moon traveler from a place where he is in maximum harmony with the weather. With no weather on the moon, your mood would never change. Imagine the dangerous implications of a man leaving from Pittsburgh on a rainy December day and being forever fixed with that earth mood upon him. I suggest that all moon travelers be launched from Alabama on an April morning when even the meanest mortal feels ten feet tall.

I wonder if they would like my advice at Canaveral.

Love, Mama

GBANGBAMA
OCTOBER

Dear Lolly and Suzy,

I shouldn't complain about the amount of mail I receive as I probably have a steadier supply than anyone in Sierra Leone. The housemother forces Tom and Rob to write to their parents every Sunday and Suzy writes for money with great regularity so I am assured of three letters a week.

I was looking through the mailbag with Bob today and found five copies of *Soviet News* addressed to five of our few literate employees. This is a small weekly paper published by the Soviet Embassy in London and is available "free on request." I found the paper excruciatingly boring and repetitious. Here is an example of the material: "The revolutionary principles of the American Declaration of Independence are buried in oblivion. Those who vigorously uphold the principles of the Declaration of Independence are now frequently imprisoned." This quote was from a congratulatory message sent to the United States for our Fourth of July. The only amusing line which I found in the paper was written in large type: "REPRODUCTION OF THIS MATTER IN PART OR IN FULL IS PERMITTED."

Think of the amount of money Russia is spending on propaganda if five copies of this paper are sent to a place as remote and insignificant as Gbangbama. Africans cannot afford to subscribe to anything unless it is free. It is even a sacrifice to buy a stamp to get their name on the free Soviet mailing list. I wish we could get some of our surplus magazines and papers into the hands of people who are crying for something to read or to look at. Everywhere I looked in America was a stack of magazines or papers waiting for an overladen garbage man. I wish our government would sponsor a program for the American housewife to send all her surplus literature to the bushman. Magazines and newspapers would hurry his progress into the twentieth century. He could look at them, use them to paper his house, stuff his mattress, diaper his baby and sometimes even read them. Our capitalist literature is infinitely more colorful and attractive than the communist variety, and the African would always choose ours if he had the chance.

Bob had to go down to Bonthe yesterday on business and by chance we met an entomologist there. He is pursuing African rhinoceros beetles to see if they have parasites. He is from New Caledonia in the Pacific, and there the beetles destroy the oil palms. The African beetle is harmless to the oil palm and he is trying to find out why. As a sideline he gathers up interesting pets, his current interest being Olivia, a huge tarantula spider. He told us that the sure way to tell a tarantula from other spiders was to notice their jaws. Tarantulas bite up and down and other spiders bite crossways like pinchers. The entomologist also said that the only way a tarantula could kill anyone was to scare them to death. Their venom is no worse than a wasp's. I have so much to learn. And I am so prejudiced. I didn't believe a word that man said about tarantulas.

Love, Mama

Dear Lolly and Suzy,

Bob came from Freetown yesterday and brought me two presents which made me as happy as the day we burned the mortgage. They were two grubby, weathered, grotesque little soapstone figurines. They are Nomoli, rare and old carved figures that are buried in the farms to bring good crops. Genuine ones are not the product of any existing tribes though they all revere and use them when they find them. African craftsmen are capable of counterfeiting any object desired by European collectors and the fact that these didn't cost anything is the most favorable proof of their authenticity. A geologist dug several up in the bush near Liberia and gave these two to Bob.

A Nigerian trader in Freetown has a dozen "Benin Bronzes" in his back room which he keeps trying to sell us for a hundred dollars each. He says his pickins dug them up in Eastern Nigeria. We are tempted when we consult our books about African bronzes because these look genuine. Then we think of the generations of British collectors who have combed West Africa and we remember the talent of the African trader for outwitting the hapless white man and we reconsider.

Probably the best examples of African art which we have acquired are some masks that we bought from the Bundu and Congoli devil dancers in Gbangbama. They are certainly authentic because we have seen them in use. If the devil isn't

195

too lazy to carve himself another, he will sell you the one he is wearing when he finishes his ceremony. The mask is sacred only when it is being used for a certain purpose, so if the eccentric white man wants to give him ten shillings for a desanctified mask, why not?

All of African art is connected with their religion. The mask is a representation of a spirit-deity. The masks are grotesque, sometimes having animal as well as human features—a deity can't be expected to have an ordinary run-of-the-mill face. The dancer by his skill is supposed to evoke the presence of the spirit which his mask represents. As a precaution against the evoked spirit taking complete possession of him, the dancer is fully clothed, with stockinged feet and gloved hands, so no part of him will be exposed.

I have a Sierra Leone musical instrument called a balangi which I think is a work of art. It is like a marimba, consisting of a series of bars made of hard, resonant wood which are played by two wooden mallets with lumps of crude rubber on the end. The resonators underneath the bars are made of small gourds containing various-sized holes with cobwebs pasted over them. I can play a perfect scale on it except for one sour note. I can't wait to get the balangi home and walk into a music store and ask them to tune it for me. Should they take a saw or a piece of sandpaper to the bars? Should the gourd holes be reduced or enlarged? Perhaps the spider webs need to be cleaned and glazed? A fascinating prospect.

Everyone at camp is busy getting their photographic equipment ready for the Queen's visit. The talk is of 16-mm. movies, 8-mm. movies, light meters, tripods, Zoom lenses and all sorts of things that I don't understand. I am the only one with a box Brownie and I think they are hard to beat. I gather from all this camera talk around that camera manufacturers are beginning to wise up. The newest and most expensive cameras are very simple to operate. You simply point at the object you want to take and snap. This is exactly what I have always done with my box Brownie.

Love, Mama

GBANGBAMA<br/>NOVEMBER

Dear Lolly and Suzy,

Pussy cat, pussy cat, where have you been? We've been to Bo to visit the Queen. Yesterday was the great day and we and the six other Europeans at camp drove over to spend the day at the durbar. Bo is only sixty miles but we had to get up at five thirty to be off in time. Laden with cameras, deck chairs, umbrellas, thermos bottles and food, we drove to the Jong and crossed by dugout canoes to the Land Rovers which we had taken across the day before. Our Sunday clothes were carefully wrapped in towels inside a suitcase to protect them from the thick red dust. The rainy season ended about two weeks ago and the roads are full of thick, choking dust, stirred up by the unusual amount of traffic. We detoured by the village of Dodo as the other road was closed for the Queen's private use. (I saw nothing unusual in Dodo, only a few conventional chickens.)

We spent the day in a friend's house which overlooked the Royal Route and the durbar field. After unloading all our paraphernalia we settled down in his yard to eat our lunch and watch the crowds go by. Bob got up on top of the Land Rover and set up his tripod to take a few pictures but he found the subjects so grand and varied that he stayed there all day. Occasionally we offered him an umbrella for shade or a sandwich or a drink but he never came down until late in the afternoon.

197

We decorated the outside of the house with British, French and American flags and our host, good Scotsman that he was, ripped down a blue curtain and pinned some strips from an old sheet on it and made a fine St. Andrew's Cross to hang beside our flags. All morning thousands of people—chiefs, dancers and devils, arrayed in beautiful, bizarre and colorful costumes—streamed past to take their place on the field and wait for the Queen. By comparison all the white people looked very drab and dowdy except for the Queen and the Duke. They drove by in an open Rolls Royce, she wearing a pale-pink dress and a tiara of pearls and he in a sparkling white naval uniform. She was thoughtful to wear a tiara on a hot afternoon as we would have been bitterly disappointed with a queen without jewels.

The Queen and her party sat in a small stand beside the durbar field where all forty-five of the chiefs in our province were presented to her. Each chief was allowed a retinue of about thirty people, the elite of the chiefdom, farmers, hunters, fishermen, dancers and his favorite wives and children. He was carried in a hammock slung from a canopy which was carried on the heads of four stalwart dancers. They pranced along with a brisk step while the chiefs looked calm and dignified. I feared for their safety, especially as some of them were so old and fragile that they would have shattered like glass had they been dropped. One lady chief was over eighty years old and there were several men that old. I took some excellent pictures of Madam Titti Messy looking very regal in a pink robe with an attendant blowing a carved elephant tusk and two children on either side fanning her with palm fans. Every male chief carried a generous white cloth to wipe the sweat from his brow as his heavy country-cloth robe was as hot as a blanket. The parade passed across the field for several hours, dancing all the way. Dancing is the chief art form of Africa and the people expressed all their activities in dances—planting their crops, rowing their canoes and harvesting their rice. Women sat on platforms on the heads of dancers, spinning their cotton and preparing their rice. A small deer in a cage, a property of the hunter's dance, escaped to the delight of the audience. When a retinue arrived in front of the Queen, the chief was presented and the best solo dancers performed for her. I saw several new dances which I had not seen before, some dancing in fire and others slashing themselves with knives. (I got some gorgeous bloody pictures.) One soloist was supported on his navel on a pole six inches in diameter. The pole was on a platform carried by four bearers so he was about twelve feet in the air. His head, arms and legs were covered with a raffia costume and the wild gyrations he went through made him look like a caterpillar on a hot griddle. Many devils wore huge raffia costumes and looked like mobile haystacks.

The thing that impressed me most at the durbar was the carnival atmosphere and the universal good humor of the crowd, my first experience of the unity that royalty can evoke. The Premier is a Mende from this province so of course everyone was honoring him, too. Every Mende did his best with joy and enthusiasm and they really know how to put on a show.

We are the only American company represented here so we got invitations to the reception which the governor gave for the Queen. The invitations were as rare as hen's teeth and I will frame mine to hang in the parlor at Bugtussle. I took five handkerchiefs along in my handbag to have them hallowed by being in The Presence and I will send them to my little nieces at Christmas.

Bob and I bathed and dressed after the durbar and drove to the reception in the Humber Super Snipe which we use for state occasions. It looked fine even though the muffler is gone and it roars like a 707 jet and there is a good crop of mushrooms growing on the floor, a legacy of the rainy season. Kamara was our chauffeur, wearing a dazzling new green fez in place of his usual large-brimmed brown felt. With all the exotic headgear in Africa I don't know where he got that old brown felt that makes him look like a private eye. I warned him not to wear that hat to see the Queen, expecting him to turn up in his chauffeur's cap rather than the green fez.

The reception was uncrowded and pleasant with the Queen and Duke wandering among the guests. I followed her around for an hour breathing down her neck and memorizing her clothes and jewels to describe to you. The Provincial Commissioner said that he would present us if we stood in the right place (which we did) but just as the Queen came by a huge chieftainess oozed up, eclipsed me completely and took my place in history. She was presented while I peered over her shoulder and counted pearls on the royal neck.

The Queen is gracious and pretty with a beautiful figure and skin like peaches and cream. As she walks through a crowd her standard bearer walks a few paces behind carrying her personal flag. This is a great help at garden parties because one can always tell when she is near and stop munching sandwiches and adjust one's girdle should the flag come in one's direction.

The Commissioner and his wife had dinner with the Queen that evening. To an Englishman this is equivalent to a trip to Mecca and he can now die happy. The Commissioner had worked very hard on preparations for the visit. It is hard to find accommodations of any kind in the bush, much less accommodations for the world press and the royal party. Besides the Queen and the Duke there were two ladies-in-waiting, a dresser and an assistant dresser for the Queen, two maids for the ladies-in-waiting, a hairdresser for the Queen and six footmen and two pages, a valet for the Duke, secretaries for everybody and representatives from the Army, Navy, Air

Forces and Scotland Yard. None of these people are the kind that can sleep on the studio couch.

The reception seemed so relaxed and informal that it is hard to realize that the Queen is probably closer guarded than any person on earth. We and our invitations were scrutinized at three separate points, the last check being made by the head of the CID himself.

It was a marvelous day and worth coming back across the Jong by canoe at midnight in the pitch dark. With our Land Rover full of gear, we had forgotten a flashlight.

Love, Mama

GBANGBAMA

CHRISTMAS

Dear Lolly and Suzy,

Another sad Christmas with three-fifths of my children absent, a thin homemade Christmas tree with tarnished decorations and hot, miserable weather. But Tom and Rob enjoyed it. With no other children to make odious comparisons, they didn't realize they had a frugal Christmas. For their chief present I bought a big supply of fireworks in Freetown, left over from Guy Fawkes Day which the English celebrate in November. Fireworks, properly used, are the finest present boys can get. Properly used means for parents to ignore how, when and where they will be fired. I told Tom and Rob that they were big boys now and could be trusted to shoot fireworks sensibly; then I retired behind a brick wall for the next few days. They blasted away until the last infernal device was used up, singeing the cat, igniting Mr. Beattie's verandah, setting fire to the grass and grazing the head of Mr. Ryter with one erratic rocket. The worst casualty was a few burned

201

fingers for Rob. Tom being older and wiser let him put off the most daring shots.

Before Christmas we were invited down to the village school for their yearly program. Bob was asked to announce the numbers and had to pronounce such names as Kongyemi, Lahai, Kpangebagbele, Gbap and Kali. The program was excellent, with enthusiastic and uninhibited performances all around. The children from five to thirteen were born actors. They recited "Twinkle Twinkle Little Star," "The Death of Arthur," "Little Jack Horner" and Shakespeare's "Seven Ages of Man" in precise, perfect English without understanding a word of what they were saying. Then came the best part of the program, several plays written in Mende by the schoolmaster depicting every phase of local life in the raw. The audience and the actors were as one and shared every emotion. Unhampered by the fact that this was a Protestant mission school, all the plays were filled with drunkenness. The children staggered around drinking palm wine out of gourds, imitating their elders at their favorite diversion. The audience laughed with delight. Idiots and cripples were portrayed by the children with startling conviction. One small boy had a huge calabash tied under his clothes to represent a bulging hernia. This was a great hit with the villagers but I felt a bit queasy because there was a real hernia victim nearby. In another play a child was brought in on a board as a stiff corpse. Others in the cast acted out a few brisk, business-like scenes then proceeded to dig a grave and bury him. I wish I could have understood what they were saying. After the plays we sang a few carols and the national anthem and were dismissed. What dull grammar-school programs we have in America.

Every Yuletide the people come up the hill from the village to sing and dance for us and hold out their hands for their Christmas dash. After about the twentieth group of dancers our dashes get pretty meager. A group is outside now dancing around Rob chanting and rattling their shake-shakes. Every now and then I can hear the word "manager, manager, manager" in their chant. They are probably singing, "The manager is an old slob. He gave us only two bob." Two bob is twenty-eight cents and that is exactly what he gave the last group.

Love, Mama

Dear Lolly and Suzy,

I am making all sorts of resolutions for this new year, now that I am going to be a grandmother. It will be so strange to have a baby around that isn't mine.

Me a grandma! Incredible. I feel so young it always gives me a jolt to see that crumbling visage staring out of the looking glass. I keep telling myself that I am younger than Rita Hayworth. Why hasn't her physical plant begun to give way as mine has? Does she spend half an hour poking at an invisible needle with an invisible thread when she wants to do a little mending?

In days past when I dropped a dime under the bed, I immediately crawled under and retrieved it. Now I resort to all sorts of devious strategy, calling one of the children, poking hopefully under the spread with the toe of my shoe or getting the dust mop and making wide sweeps back and forth—anything rather than crawling under and using my stiff muscles.

A year ago I had no sympathy for people who wore glasses —I never thought of them one way or another. Now I realize how callous I've been—and how ignorant. Splendid invention that they are, glasses still take a bit of study and experimen-

203

tation to use them to maximum advantage. First I used them only for threading a needle, then for reading fine print, then I found that they could be used profitably for playing bridge. The clarity of my cards increased tenfold but the other players seemed to be swimming in mushroom soup. Now I find that bifocals will solve this problem. When I learn how to wear bifocals and how to lie on my side and read in bed without knocking them off I will have the eye problem licked.

My shape is another thing to which I have given some thought. I don't seem to indent around the middle anymore. Unlike Miss Hayworth, I have a more or less straight line from shoulder to hip. If I can adopt an old-world attitude toward this it will be a great comfort. One thing Europeans find so disconcerting about American women is that they all have the same shape. It is a beautiful one, mind you, but the same. Europeans find it unsettling to get a rear view of a svelte 36-24-36 lady and have her turn around and be someone's grandmother. Their ladies come in three sizes—Very Young, Young and Mature. I am going to be the Mature type—soft with a bit of give. What child wants to snuggle up to a hard grandma with perfect muscular tone?

Bob says he has no particular worries about being a grandfather. The worst aspect of the situation is that he is afraid he will lose face by living with a grandmother. Rob is elated at the prospect of being an uncle. There is not a single uncle in his school.

Love, Mama

Dear Lolly and Suzy,

I have been sick with dyspepsia for ten days. It is nothing serious—I am just beginning to come apart gently. I have to carry stomach pills around in my purse. It is so humiliating. I could recover if I could get the cook to cease and desist from using so much fat in his cooking. Africans love fat because their diet is eternally lacking it. The cook even fills the pan with grease to fry bacon.

I think I will start doing my own cooking now that we have a new gas stove. Gbangbama is getting so modern it is embarrassing. We invite our friends up from Freetown to see the *real* bush and there is our new stove, a deep freezer and a pink washing machine staring them in the face.

There are five of the new stoves at camp now and we are trying to teach the cooks to use the bottled gas without blowing us off the hill. My cook blows out the flame when he is finished with the burner but the pilot light confounds him by making it pop on again. The oven doesn't have a pilot light and he turns it on full blast then fumbles around for a few minutes to light the match. I can always tell when dinner is being started by the WHOOM that comes rolling out of the kitchen. I have tried to teach Luceni that escaping gas has a terrible smell so he will be alert to the danger. I went in the kitchen one morning and smelled gas and said, "Luceni, do you smell something?" He said, "Yes, Madam," and pointed to the kitten's sand box. I said, "No, not that." Then he beckoned me to come outside the kitchen where he showed me the hen's roost. I will never convince him that our shiny new stove stinks.

I have just cleaned up the guesthouse and found a bottle of Selsun left by an Australian visitor. This is a remedy for scalp ailments which gets around as much as Kilroy. Bob was prescribed a bottle by a dermatologist in Florida who was so high class and expensive that we were sure his treatments were unique. A few weeks later I saw some in Alabama on Tommy's bathroom shelf. My brother in Virginia had a bottle and traveling further, I found the ubiquitous bottle in a Madrid hotel. Now to find it in the African bush belonging to an Australian makes me wonder. Is there an international brotherhood of dermatologists? I don't like dermatologists. They should all turn into general practitioners where they can do some good. This treating skin ailments is for the birds. When people are homesick or in debt or hate their mother-in-law, the skin is the first thing that outwardly rebels—a rash here, an itch there etc. Dermatologists waste their time and your money trying to get rid of the rash when they should get rid of the mother-in-law. I am always breaking out but it never lasts very long. Your father just says firmly, "No, you can't have a sable coat," or "European children *never* get yaws," or "Suzy and Lolly CANNOT come for Christmas," and the rash goes away.

Love, Mama

GBANGBAMA<br>JANUARY

Dear Lolly and Suzy,

We have four new bearded neighbors: Henri, Klaus, Romain and Michel. They belong to a Swiss firm which is mining bauxite about thirty miles from Gbangbama. They invited us to a party to celebrate the betrothal or the wedding of Romain. Because of the language difficulty we aren't sure which. They speak German, French, Italian and Romansch.

The party was held in a temporary house that two of the

bachelors have built in a dank swamp where they will build their ore-shipping facilities in the future. It was a casual, Florida-type house built of rough boards and thatch with a tree growing out the middle. The place was low and damp but there wasn't a single mosquito. As Rob says, they were all married with families. The English ladies were nearly eaten alive but my fortified Florida blood doesn't attract mosquitoes. Having been bitten for over forty years, I am immune. Nobody believed me when I told them that the mosquitoes were twice as bad at Bugtussle as in this African swamp.

The bachelors' house gets cut off from the mainland when the tide comes in and to get home you have to walk two hundred yards across a pole bridge with black, crocodile-infested water below. If the poles were laid crosswise it would be a simple matter to walk across, but they are lashed together lengthwise and your feet slip between the poles, twisting your ankles and making the whole bridge wobble like jelly.

In spite of these trivial inconveniences we had a marvelous party. Henri played his guitar and sang "Swanee River," "Hang Down Your Head, Tom Dooley," and "O Susannah" in French. Michel climbed fifteen feet up in the tree to his hammock and went to sleep. I don't know why he hangs his hammock so high, perhaps a vain attempt to get away from the mosquitoes. Caesar, a gay, white-haired caballero from South America, did a cha-cha. Don't ask how a Latin got in this Swiss gathering. This kind of thing is commonplace in Africa. There was also a Pole at the party doing a mazurka.

Henri, the host, was a vegetarian, so for dinner the pièce de résistance was a ten-pound Gouda cheese. He cut it in half and placed the cut sides toward a charcoal fire. When the sides softened he would scrape the cheese off into our waiting plates. With potatoes, pickles, vin du jour and fresh pineapple for dessert we had a delicious dinner.

About ten o'clock we were offered a boat ride in the new launch which had just been sent out to survey the river channel. We got on the launch and they opened it up full throttle. We went zooming up Gbangbama creek in the pitch dark with mangrove limbs lashing us as we sped past. The channel is full of granite boulders and sandbanks and I knew this intemperate speed boded woe. An African boy was at the helm and I took some comfort from this, thinking that at least he knew the channel. He looked so confident skimming along at fifteen knots. Bill Rose told me later that his sole mechanical experience, until he was appointed launch captain through his forged papers, had been as a helper on one of our drilling crews.

We got home safely after a fine party but I do think that, as yachtsmen, the Swiss should stick to skiing.

Love, Mama

My dear two-generation family,

The cable came today announcing our grandchild but you didn't say whether it was a boy or a girl! Either Tommy was too excited to think of the sex or the cable was garbled in Freetown.

It doesn't matter just so everyone is fine. I ran out to meet the mailman as I have been doing for weeks and when he gave me the cable I read it and burst into tears. All the Africans were so upset until I explained that I was just crying for joy and relief that everything went well.

The chief clerk in the office just came down with an official delegation of workers and said that they wanted to congratulate your father and from now on his official title would be Pa Spencer. They were very serious about this as Pa is a term of great respect among the Africans.

I shall be Ma Spencer hereafter even though a delegation has neglected to notify me officially.

I will be waiting impatiently to find out if my grandchild is Glenn or Elizabeth.

Love, love, love, Mama

Dear Lolly and Suzy,

Your father is elated with a grandson. I hope you all are pleased. When John was born someone asked Suzy how she liked her little brother and she said, "Oh, I love him to pieces but I am so afraid he will grow up to be a little boy!" Anyway, I like little boys.

Bob says we can go on leave after Tom and Rob's spring holiday. Amadu and I drove to Kabala to get them yesterday. Amadu is from the north and he is always happy to leave the low bush country and visit his brothers in Kabala. The fact that he can buy clabber there influences him, too. There are many cows up there, and the ladies all sell clabber from big pans on their heads. Amadu carried two empty pails from Gbangbama to put his clabber in. I told him that I ate this delicacy when I was a small girl in Alabama, clabber with a spoonful of sugar on it. This is exactly how the Fulas eat it if they can afford the sugar.

The missionaries were at Kabala to collect their children, so we heard a variety of news from every part of the country. An eight-foot cobra was killed at the Kamakwie Wesleyan

Hospital. The doctor's wife has hepatitis. Three hundred people a week are treated at their leper clinic. An eye surgeon from America is coming out, at his own expense, to do surgery for the hospital for two months. An American dentist has already come, at his expense, to fix all the missionaries' teeth. (I am going to write a fan letter to such nice men.)

The missionary from up on the Guinea border has a bongo skin. A bongo is a rare African antelope. He is so big (according to Tom) that he looks like a cow on stilts. The missionary from Yefin now has to walk only twelve miles to get to a road. The last time I talked to her she had to walk twenty-five miles.

On the way to Kabala I stopped by a friend's house in Magburaka and her husband had killed an elephant the day before. The huge tusks and a foot were in front of her door smelling to high heaven. I had myself photographed with the trophies but afterward I felt a little ashamed. I hate for things to be killed, especially anything with such a magnificent foot. The feet are used to make waste baskets or umbrella stands.

The Kabala school had an end-of-term program for the parents. They had a play about Abe Lincoln's father and his second marriage. Tom played the part of the circuit rider who married Mr. Lincoln and Mrs. Johnston and conducted Nancy Hanks's funeral on the same day. Nancy had died the year before, but there had been no preacher to hold her funeral. Tom was a brisk, business-like parson who urged the characters to move along with things as he had several weddings and funerals to conduct before nightfall. Tom was impressed when I told him that one of his great-great-grandfathers was a **real** circuit rider.

Tom and Rob like Kabala better than any school they have ever attended and even hate to leave it for a holiday. The school does rather neglect current events but perhaps this is for the best. Tom didn't know Glenn had flown around the world the week before. Yes-ss, he knew he was going but he didn't know just when.

We found plenty of palaver when we got back to Gbang-bama. One of the laborers has been selling our tires to the village lorry owner. The lorry came up the hill and we recognized our numbered tires. Now another faithful employee has been sacked.

Europeans are always laying traps to catch "teefing" Africans. They must or nothing would continue to function in the country. But I hate to catch a thief. I am so embarrassed when mankind doesn't measure up that I always want to look the other way. I am even embarrassed when I see a poor television show or a bad movie. I feel that I am somehow to blame. I must be carrying the greatest burden of guilt in the history of mankind if I feel responsible for Hollywood and television and the bushman's honesty.

Love, Mama

GBANGBAMA

MARCH

Dear Lolly and Suzy,

We are almost through packing. I have the manuscript of my precious African journal in a safe place with my passport and my handbag. I have lost it twice in the past year so I will not let it out of my hands until I submit it to a publisher. I shrink at the thought of turning my tender work over to the harsh scrutiny of some editor. They are intelligent, merciless people who know the difference between frogs and toads, moths and butterflies and stalactites and stalagmites. They can spell, too.

Tom, Rob and I are going home two months before your father's leave is due. I hate to leave him all alone but I cannot wait two months to see my grandson. Bob will be too busy to miss us anyway. They have found a fine deposit of rutile and he is making plans to build a pilot plant for mining. It is just as well that I have begun to feel at home in Africa because I think Bob will be here for years.

But I have learned so much that I am prepared to stay here until your father retires. To live in Africa with equanimity one must follow a simple rule: Don't worry about things! Plan to be wet in the wet season and dry in the dry season and don't fight the bugs. Peaceful coexistence, that's the philosophy.

Love, Mama